Stage Management Basics

Without assuming any intrinsic prior knowledge of the theatrical field and its associated, specialized terminology, *Stage Management Basics* takes a look at every aspect of stage management; from reading a script for the first time to opening night protocols, including how to meet with directors and theater staff, running auditions, best practices in communication, and much more. Additionally, this book features multiple appendices containing stage management form templates, blank versions of which are available on its companion website, and an American to English (UK) glossary. This book touches on the basic principles of stage management that are found in theatre, dance, and opera productions.

Emily Roth is a freelance stage manager and production manager currently living and working in New York City. She holds a BA from Coe College in Theatre with an emphasis in Design and Technology and has worked professionally over the last three years across the Midwest and New York, primarily as a stage manager, but also as a lighting designer, electrician, sound designer, and props master. As an early career professional that is largely self-taught in stage management, Emily felt the need for a text that introduces the topics that everyone takes for granted in young stage managers.

Jonathan Allender-Zivic, M.F.A., has been teaching and working in the theatrical industry for over 15 years primarily a Professor, Lighting Designer, and Technical Director. Jonathan is an Assistant Professor of Theatre at the University of South Dakota. Jonathan has over 125 professional and academic credits in the past 5 years, keeping an active hand in the professional arena; he has most recently worked regionally in the Midwest designing lights, but over the course of the past 15 years he has worked all over the country with different theatres and taught at four different colleges and university since receiving his MFA from Western Illinois University.

Katy McGlaughlin has been working in and around theatre her whole life; mostly stage managing and a little bit of everything else. She has worked all across the United States on productions ranging from new works to large-scale musicals and dance. She also spent some time as an assistant production manager and a company manager. Katy holds a BFA from Webster University, where she specialized in stage management and technical direction. After many years in the professional arena, Katy is pursuing her MFA in stage management at the University of Iowa to allow her to continue on to future academic endeavors.

Stage Management Basics

A Primer for Performing Arts Stage Managers

EMILY ROTH

JONATHAN ALLENDER-ZIVIC

KATY McGLAUGHLIN

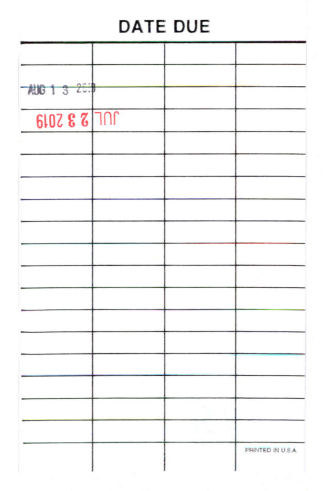

First published 2017
by Routledge
711 Third Avenue, New York, NY 10017

and by Routledge
2 Park Square, Milton Park, Abingdon, Oxon OX14 4RN

Routledge is an imprint of the Taylor & Francis Group, an informa business

Library of Congress Cataloging in Publication Data
Names: Allender-Zivic, Jonathan, author. | Roth, Emily, author. | McGlaughlin, Katy, author.
Title: Stage management basics : a primer for performing arts stage managers /
    Jonathan Allender-Zivic, Emily Roth, Katy McGlaughlin.
Description: New York : Routledge, 2016. | Includes bibliographical references and index.
Identifiers: LCCN 2016006671 | ISBN 9781138960558 (hbk : alk. paper) | ISBN 9781138960541
    (pbk : alk. paper) | ISBN 9781315660257 (ebk : alk. paper)
Subjects: LCSH: Stage management—Handbooks, manuals, etc.
Classification: LCC PN2086 .A45 2016 | DDC 792.02/5—dc23
LC record available at http://lccn.loc.gov/2016006671

ISBN: 978-1-138-96055-8 (hbk)
ISBN: 978-1-138-96054-1 (pbk)
ISBN: 978-1-315-66025-7 (ebk)

Typeset in Minion
by Apex CoVantage, LLC

Dedication

We want to pass along our experiences and love for the art to you, the reader, in hopes of kindling your excitement and passion to start and continue a life in the field of theatre.

Contents

Acknowledgments

To all those people throughout our lives and careers that have guided, mentored, taught, and influenced us.

Introduction

By Jonathan Allender-Zivic

As a theatrical educator in both small and large academic settings I have to say that, to me, one of the most neglected fields of instruction is stage management. Everyone assumes students know what is needed and expected of them. We rely on them to execute and complete tasks that most students don't have the faintest idea how to do correctly, let alone without any guidance or mentorship. Good stage management is pivotal to a successful production process. This text has been created to help fill in the gaps for programs where a specific stage management track or emphasis does not exist or for those who wish to get a good grasp of the basics.

The purpose of this book is to help beginning young and less experienced stage managers grasp the enormous number of tasks that will be expected of them as the stage manager of a production. So often experienced theatrical practitioners forget that terms and processes that are second nature to them are not as clear and clean cut to students that are often thrown into these positions. When laying out this book, we tried to go back to the basic building blocks, and explain everything as if this is your first time ever working in a theater. This step-by-step approach will build a strong foundation for you to work from with a solid basis in terminology and processes. This book is not meant to focus on only the professional or academic world, but also to give a generic overview of the field, and should serve as guidelines and a starting place for inexperienced stage managers.

It is important to note at this time that there are already many different textbooks in existence for the field of stage management. No single book will agree on every method. There are many different types of theaters out there with many different artistic structures, all of which function slightly or not so slightly differently. That being said, this book is another view compiled from three different professionals who have worked in different theaters, positions, and environments, each with different training and experiences. We have strived to pool our knowledge of a wide variety of theaters and create a starting point for you to get your feet and maybe your knees wet, but not drown. The methods in this book are not the only correct methods, and everything in the theatrical environment needs to be flexible to a point. However, standardization is also important, so use your best judgment as you begin to grow as a stage manager to decide when to bend and change the "rules." The words "typically" and "usually" are used a lot in this text because we are talking about best practices and past experiences. Always remain open to trying and learning new things during what is hopefully an extremely collaborative process.

One thing that I do not think can be stressed enough is communication. Always communicate—it is better to over-communicate than under-communicate—always ask questions, share information, and make it easily accessible. There will be people who are upset by being included in an e-mail they don't really need to be on, but it's better that they have the information and not need it than not have the information and need it. Stage management is not only a job, but also a state of mind. It requires dedication, passion, patience, a little neuroticism, and a whole lot of love for what you do.

Chapter One

The Psychology of Stage Managing

Being a good stage manager requires organization, structure, and communication. These are often the most discussed and well-outlined facets of the job. However, maintaining paperwork and coordinating the show is just a portion. A large aspect of stage management is the personal interaction between stage manager and all others involved in the process. A stage manager is one of the few individuals with whom all members of the company interact and, as such, becomes a confidant, a coach, a peacekeeper, and a friend. Actors will approach the stage manager when they are having issues with their fellow actors, the designers, or, in particular, with their director. Anticipate becoming the shoulder for them to cry on, someone to vent to, and a confidant of any personal life troubles that may interfere with their work or the production. In all of this, you should be a source of comfort and confidentiality, but remain neutral. It should be your goal to help them through an issue by listening and finding a compromise or a civil solution. Never gossip about fellow company members or encourage exclusion. Theatre is all about collaboration and any steps away from that will end poorly.

These people skills, like any other aspect of stage management, are acquired. With experience, you will improve and you will begin to learn how to read the people you work with and better anticipate problems and possible solutions.

Qualities of a Good Stage Manager

Organization

As evidenced by the stage manager's responsibilities outlined throughout this book, organization is one of the most obvious and easily identifiable qualities necessary in a stage manager. Good organization leads to an overall smoother process and is something to strive for in building your stage management toolkit. However, it is not the only quality and not even necessarily the most important.

Attention to Detail

Just as important as organization is a keen attention to detail. This will be critical in making sure all the tiniest elements of the show are addressed properly and also to maintain the integrity of the show once it has opened. The stage manager must notice when a piece of furniture is off its spike (not in its correct position), if a light cue is incorrect, or if an actor is seconds late for an entrance, as it may affect the entire performance. In rehearsal, this allows you to assist the director with continuity and helps with tracking and run paperwork. Attention to detail is also part of the psychology of stage managing: being aware of the subtle shifts and changes of the company will allow you to gauge tempers, address needs before they become problematic, and keep the company running happily.

Compassion

Beyond being personal secretary to the whole production team, the stage manager also steps into the role of psychologist, mediator, friend, and parent. Those who work in theatre, especially actors and directors (and even designers!), make their living from exposing themselves, physically and emotionally, through their art. Because of this, they tend to be more sensitive than the average Joe. You may become their confidant and the more compassion you show, the more they will be able to resolve "offstage," rather than allowing their personal issues to come through onstage or in the rehearsal room. You may feel like their parent, but they will thank you for being willing to hold their hand and respect you all the more for your patience and confidence. This is a careful line to walk because compassion and patronization are similar and too far to one side can create a bigger monster. It is important to remember that respect is a large part of compassion; when people make themselves vulnerable they need to know that they are safe and will not be judged. It is also your responsibility to keep the show going and, as far as the job goes, that is more important than being friends; work with compassion but don't be a doormat.

Confidence

In order to gain the trust of the rest of the company members, all stage managers must conduct their work with confidence. The artistic choices of the production, the safety of the personnel, and the execution of many, specific, and detailed items are the stage manager's responsibility. Confidence in one's own work inspires confidence and trust from those working with you. This does not mean, however, that you need to have all the answers or do everything correctly the first time. As with everything in life, stage management is a continuous learning process and mistakes happen. However, uncertainty, doubt, and the inability to stick to your guns will only hinder your ability to connect with the company members in the ways necessary to facilitate a successful production. Any uncertainty regarding your job should be handled on a one-on-one basis as much as possible, be it with a stage management mentor unassociated with the production, the producer, or the director. It is okay to not have all the answers, but it is better in the moment to make a decision and stick with it, even if it turns out to be the wrong decision. A lack of confidence is viewed as a weakness and too much will severely limit the stage manager's ability to control the rehearsal room. Find a balance: don't become cocky and overconfident, even if you really do have all the answers. It takes just as much confidence and earns respect to admit you are wrong, but there are appropriate times and places to do so.

When giving maintenance notes, give only necessary notes and don't be overly nitpicky or you will risk losing the confidence and trust of the actors and technicians and they will more easily dismiss you.

Poise

Whether in the stress of final dress when half the costumes are incomplete and the lead actor has yet to learn their lines correctly, or in rehearsal when a prop accidentally breaks while twelve people are asking you questions and you are trying to track down a missing actor, it is critical to have the ability to address issues calmly and rationally, without allowing strong emotions to take over. This ability will help you gain the trust of your company. The stage manager's role is, among other things, to be the stability and voice of reason in the company. If they see this waver or fall apart, it can quickly cause panic within the company. When first starting out, it's okay for a stage manager's inner composure to waver, but try to never let that affect the outer composure that is the public face of the leader. If, for some reason, you do lose your temper, recover it as quickly as you can; don't let it color the rest of the process. A lot can be gained by apologizing, publicly if necessary.

Adaptability

Many stage managers are control freaks, and often it is a helpful trait. However, the desire to control all of the details must be tempered with the ability to adapt. It is easy in the midst of a long tech week to get frustrated that we fell short of the day's goal but a good stage manager will put aside that frustration and help the team re-evaluate the goals for the next day; a great stage manager will do it with good humor and a smile. Shows are living breathing creatures; you never know what is going to change but being able to assimilate the information and keep moving is critical. This trait also shows itself in the stage manager's ability to work in different venues, with different companies and different creative teams—adapting to the different needs and styles of your director, creative team, and cast will allow you to be in control of any situation and to become more marketable in the industry.

> At all times during the production process, it is important to be flexible; things change, people don't show up or are sick. Roll with the punches and keep smiling.

Neutrality

One of the more difficult qualities of being a good stage manager is the ability to remain neutral in any given situation and to hold your tongue. This can be especially difficult for those who come from a directorial, acting, or design background, who are used to making design/acting decisions. The stage manager's primary role is to support and help execute the director's vision and, through that, the actors' and the designers' decisions that augment that vision. There are occasions when the director will ask for the stage manager's input regarding a decision or their opinion about an artistic choice and at that time, you can feel free to indulge them. However, this is often a trust that is gained between director and stage manager after a few instances of working together. In matters of safety it is important to speak up but do so diplomatically.

Remember that any time you are asked your opinion regarding a design choice, an acting choice, or a directing choice, your response will be a judgment on someone's art. Don't be afraid to answer honestly, but take care in your approach and your choice of words. They can hurt!

Assertiveness

The ability to show strong leadership is critical, in anything from running production meetings to maintaining focus in rehearsals, to managing and running a successful performance night after night. The stage manager is the company's steadfast leader from the first rehearsal to the closing performance and they should be able to trust you as such. Learn to find the balance between serious and fun, between compassionate friend and disciplinarian. When it comes down to it, you must be in a position to lay down the law and for them to respect you enough to listen, obey, and trust that it is for the good of the production and the good of the company as a whole. Remember that being a tyrannical dictator is not the way to do this.

Diplomacy

Stage managers need to embody all these things (confidence, leadership, organization, etc.) and also know how to talk to, interact with, and collaborate with each member of the team. There will always be a mix of personalities and it is essential to know who you can joke with, which actor prefers to be called formally, or if one designer needs to be handled with care.

Discretion

Stage managers are often privy to lots of information that isn't necessarily meant for the general population. It is of the utmost importance that the company know that the stage management team can be approached about anything and they will deal with it respectfully, quietly, and professionally. It is important to have a trusted person not related to the production or company with whom you can discuss ideas or challenges. Trust is hard won and easily lost; remember, discretion is the better part of valor.

A Sense of Humor

Theatre is very serious business . . . to those in the business of theatre. Plays can (and often do) expose the rawest of human emotions and can be an incredibly stressful process. A stage manager with a good sense of humor helps to break the tension and remind everyone that they are doing this because it is fun. You are the voice of authority and will often have to be strict and unrelenting, but that doesn't mean you can't laugh along with the actor's jokes or throw out a sarcastic comment to the lighting designer during tech. There is a time and a place; be aware of your situation.

Work and Personal Satisfaction

Stage management is not a glamorous job, in any sense of the word. You will work an extraordinary number of unaccounted-for hours, produce endless pages of paperwork and reports that people won't read, and put your heart and soul into a production with rarely a "thank you" uttered. The satisfaction comes from the ability to guide a production from start to finish, with a limited number of injuries, from some text on paper to a full-fledged production. You will handle situations you have never encountered before. And you will get to work with some of the greatest, kindest, most brilliant, and most generous people in the world. It is from a job well done that you must gain satisfaction, not from applause or praise. If you are doing the job well, no one should notice it happening.

Chapter Two
Preliminary Steps

The production process can be a very hectic, fast-paced environment. Rehearsals can be extremely short (two weeks), very long (nine to ten weeks), and anywhere in between. It will depend a lot on the environment the theater is in. In the academic environment, the labor and personnel budget are not typically an issue, so the rehearsal process can be longer but the production may only run for a weekend or two. Conversely, if the theater is paying production staff and actors, then typically the process will be shortened to keep costs to a minimum. The production periods will be the exact opposite: a shorter rehearsal process and a longer run (to gain revenue). The following section talks about the steps needed to get prepared for the production process as a whole: educating oneself on the different types of theaters and theatrical terms, how to familiarize oneself with a script, start generating paperwork, and be ready to move on to the next steps in the process.

World of the Play

The world of the play sets a production in a specific context with particular rules, established by the director, to govern this specific production's concept and vision. These will guide the design team to create a cohesive production, where all of the elements fit within the world (style, concept, vision). The world of the play dictates a lot about the play, including the style (i.e., realism, expressionism, etc.) and the rules or "guidelines" (i.e., do ghosts exist?, can characters interact with them?, or are they only visible to the audience?). The world of the play is production specific, a play can be interpreted differently in each production, and the world of the play will change from production to production, i.e., Disney's *Alice in Wonderland* vs. Tim Burton's *Alice in Wonderland*.

The world of the play is typically created out of a director's concept statement or concept meetings with the director. The director takes into account many different elements and principles of theatrical structure and process. Using basic script analysis the director decides what this particular production will focus on. They analyze what the dramatic structure of the play is (the rising action, the climax, etc.), and also must have a good working knowledge of Aristotle's *The Poetics* so they can better understand the elements of the script and then in turn communicate that to the production team. The production and design team then takes this concept and any additional information and creates a visual and aural world of the play that matches the director's vision. Many times this will be a somewhat lengthy process with many conversations, revisions, and meetings.

Theaters come in all shapes and sizes, configurations and layouts, locations and areas. It is not possible to discuss all the different iterations of theaters that exist, but here are the five main types. These types may be found in buildings built expressly for the purpose of live theatre, or buildings that were modified to be theaters. Each type has its own advantages, challenges, and unique features. Being armed with this knowledge before embarking on a production will help with preparation (see Figure 2.1).

Proscenium

Proscenium theaters make up the majority of theaters in the world. With the audience only on one side of the action, and lots of space for actors to enter and scenery to live, this makes for larger scenic elements and bigger dance numbers. The oldest type of theatrical structure, the historical beginnings of the proscenium stage, started back in Greek theatre. A proscenium arch—a frame that encompasses the stage and guides the audience to the action taking place onstage—is the biggest feature of this type of theater.

Thrust

A thrust stage typically has the audience on three sides. Thrust theaters typically have smaller scenic elements because the audience needs to be able to see across the stage and large elements will obstruct their view on the sides. Some thrust theaters are old converted proscenium theaters, and still have the arch and a lot of the upstage space which can be employed for larger scenic elements, entrances and

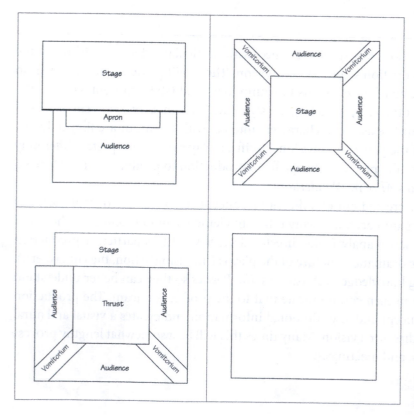

Figure 2.1 a. (top left) Proscenium Theater, b. (bottom left) Thrust Theater, c. (top right) Arena Theater, d. (bottom right) Blackbox Theater

exits, as well as storage. In the thrust environment the actors may have entrances through the audience called vomitoriums (voms for short). Many thrust theaters allow for a more intimate playgoing experience, due to the proximity of the actors to the audience. Most thrust theaters are smaller spaces, typically under 400 seats.

Arena

In arena theaters (also called "Theater in the round"), the audience surrounds the entire stage. There is no "upstage" and "downstage" but rather the action takes place in 360 degrees to cater to the whole audience. Arena theaters typically have minimal scenic elements so as not to obstruct the audience's view. Projection is being used in arena theaters with increasing frequency (to augment the existing scenery). While acting in the round the cast will always have their backs to some part of the audience.

Blackbox

A blackbox is a typically square or rectangular room usually painted completely black, hence the name. It is created to be a "flexible" space, designed to be set in any of the above configurations. A more intimate setting, most blackbox theaters seat a maximum of 200 people. Blackbox theaters, depending on the configuration, can have a wide variety of scenic elements and tend to have their own set of quirks when it comes to entrances and exits, and the storage of scenic elements.

Site-Specific or Environmental

Site-specific or environmental theatre is produced "on-location" in a venue that fits the style and vision of the production, e.g., a play about a mental hospital taking place in an old mental hospital, or a play in a bar actually happening in the local bar.

The fourth wall is the imaginary wall that exists between the audience and the actors; some productions "break" the fourth wall by interacting with the audience or bringing them into the production in some manner.

Stage Directions

In order to be able to communicate properly with the actors and the production team everyone must be speaking the same language. In theatre we use stage directions to talk about the theater, where things are happening, and where they will be going. Stage directions can take a bit of getting used to but overall one gets used to using them after a few productions and they become second nature. The most important thing to remember about stage directions is that they are always based on the actor's point of view looking toward the audience. Looking out toward the audience the actor's left becomes stage left, their right stage

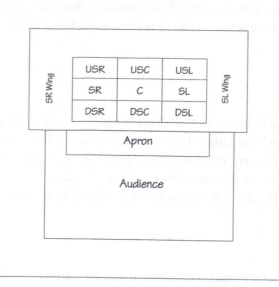

Figure 2.2 Basic Stage Directions

When working in the round (arena) sometimes it is helpful to arbitrarily choose a "downstage" to help facilitate consistency and understanding of where the actors and scenery are in a space. Using clock designations also works well, with 12 o'clock being downstage and 6 o'clock being upstage and so on.

right. Now moving away from the audience, that is called moving upstage. Historically, theaters had raked stages with the higher end farthest from the audience, meaning actors literally walked up when moving in that direction. Moving closer toward the audience is called downstage. Based on the configuration of the theater and the size of the space, these directions can be further divided into downstage right, midstage right, upstage right, etc. (see Figure 2.2).

Script

Reading the Script

The more knowledge a stage manager has about the script (and score, when applicable), the better prepared they will be for the upcoming production. As such, the very first step after being hired for a show is to obtain a copy of the script and start reading. When preparing for a production it is important to read the script a minimum of three times. This insures intimate familiarity with the script, enabling the stage manager to best serve the production . The excerpt below contains a world of information in the first few paragraphs that can really enlighten the stage manager and creative team. (see Figure 2.3).

The First Read—For Literary Purposes (Plotline, Enjoyment)

This is the time to read the script purely for its literary value, for the reader's enjoyment, and to get an overall feel for the scope and mood of the text as the audience will receive it (most audience members only see a production once, so it is important during the production that the audience gets a great

Of Mice and Men

Act 1

Scene 1

Thursday night. A sandy bank of the Salinas River sheltered with willows—one giant sycamore up R. The stage is covered with dry leaves. The feeling is sheltered and quiet. Stage is lit by a setting sun.

Curtain rises on empty stage. A sparrow is singing. There is a distant sound of ranch dogs barking aimlessly and one clear quail call. The quail call turns to a warning call and there is a beat of the flock's wings. Two figures are seen entering—L. or R., it makes no difference—in single file with GEORGE, the short man, coming in ahead of LENNIE. Both men are carrying blanket rolls. They approach the water. The small man throws down his blanket roll, the large man follows, then falls down and drinks from the river, snorting as he drinks.

George: (*Irritably.*) Lennie, for God's sake, don't drink so much. (*Leans over and shakes LENNIE.*) Lennie, you hear me! You gonna be sick like you was last night.

Lennie: (*Dips his whole head under, hat and all. As he sits on bank, his hat drips down the back.*) That's good. You drink some, George. You drink some, too.

George: (*Kneeling, dipping his fingers in water.*) I ain't sure it's good water. Looks kinda scummy to me.

Lennie: (*Imitates, dipping his finger also.*) Look at them wrinkles in the water, George. Look what I done.

George: (*Drinking from a cupped palm.*) Tastes all right. Don't seem to be runnin' much, though. Lennie, you oughtn' to drink water when it ain't running. (*Hopelessly.*) You'd drink water out of a gutter if you was thirsty. (*Throws a scoop of water into his face, rubs it around with his hand, pushes himself back and embraces his knees. LENNIE, after watching him, imitates him in every detail. GEORGE, beginning tiredly and growing angry as he speaks.*)

Figure 2.3 *Of Mice and Men* by John Steinbeck

"first read"). During this first read, don't think too much about the requirements of the script or production. That is what later readings are for. Read purely for enjoyment and understanding.

The Second Read—Preliminary Notes

This is the time to take preliminary notes, including where problem spots might be, any quick costume changes, odd set/prop/costume requirements, sound effects, etc. Note taking is different for everyone, but write either directly in the script or on a separate notepad (depending on whether it is the only copy of the script, a rented script, an electronic copy, or a full-sized copy). Note anything and everything that could impact rehearsals or the production. Always include the page number, act, and scene in these notations. You will thank yourself later on when you don't have to go back searching through your script. Color-coding the notes by department can also be helpful.

A great Excel template for preliminary notes can be found at *www.sm-sim.com/sm-kit.html*.

The Third Read—Production Analysis

A production analysis is a detailed overview of the full script, taking into account all aspects of the show (scenery, lights, sound, props, and costumes). This should be compiled on your third read-through of the script. This is the point when you add specificity to your preliminary notes (e.g., not only do you need a newspaper on page 5 but the headline should be "Extra, Extra"). As you are compiling, be sure to note relevant items both in your paperwork and in the script itself. This additional step will help immensely with initial rehearsals and keeping track of rehearsal props, sound effects, etc. Be sure to look in both the text and the stage directions; indications of these things can be given in either location (see Appendix A).

The production analysis should be a living document. Keep a copy in your promptbook for reference and keep it updated throughout the rehearsal process as things change to fit this particular production.

Textual Stage Directions

In addition to navigating the stage, the term stage directions can also refer to anything in italics in a script. These may have been written directly by the playwright with the intention that they be followed. However, just as likely, they were written by the stage manager of the first production and relate specifically to that original production. There is no guarantee that any information given in the stage directions was originally intended by the playwright or will be used by your director. For this reason, be sure to keep careful track of whether something has been indicated in the text or in the stage directions. The place to indicate this would be in the "Notes" section of the props list.

Scenery

Take note of any and all stage directions, lines, etc. that would have an effect on the scenery (including time of day, year, date, presence of windows, etc.). Additionally, take note of props and set pieces that need to be practical or functional (e.g., a window that opens or a closet that needs to hide three people). At this point in time there is no set designer involved, it is simply the information from the text. The production may end up without all scripted set pieces, but to start out and properly prepare, assume everything will exist.

Lights and Sound

Take note of any and all stage directions, lines, etc. that would have an effect on lights and/or sound (including time of day, year, date, windows, ambience, etc.). Note use of any practical lights or sounds onstage (lamp, phone, radio, etc.). Also, note any scripturally indicated lighting shifts (stage directions or text). Remember that some things affect multiple aspects of design (e.g., an open window might also require sound effects of street noise). It is especially important to mark, in your script, any sound cues that you will need to provide during rehearsal. Typically, this is any sound that affects the action of the scene (e.g., a phone ring, a doorbell, a gunshot, etc.). Ambient background sounds or soundscapes are not generally required for rehearsals.

If the script refers to the directionality of the light or sound, note this as well.

Props and Costumes

List any props and costumes indicated (either in the text or in the stage directions). Include which character(s) handles the prop or wears the costume piece and when it comes onstage and offstage. If multiple characters handle the same prop or costume piece, make a note to determine whether this will be the exact same piece or if there will need to be multiples to avoid messy tracking of the items later. This list will give you an idea of what rehearsal props you will need. Also, keep an eye out for places where quick changes, handoffs, catches, or tracking may occur and take note of these as well. Quick changes may happen between scenes or in the middle of a scene. If possible, having a few rehearsal costume pieces available is helpful.

Take particular note of hand props and personal props that are used. If it is the stage manager's responsibility to gather rehearsal/stand-in props, it will make the job that much easier.

Props

Props are considered to be anything movable or portable on a set. Any item that cannot be classified as scenery, electrics, or wardrobe falls under this category. Furniture is considered a prop in most theaters, although there are some exceptions. Props that are handled by the actors (e.g., cups, books, pencils) are known as hand props. Props that are kept in an actor's possession (e.g., pocket watches, fans, canes) are known as personal props. Items that are usually untouched by the actors (e.g., mirrors, vases, lamps, picture frames, window dressing, rugs) are known as set dressing.

If you organize these lists by character, page number, scene, etc., they will translate nicely into a preset list (or costume/prop list) later on in the process.

Some personal props may also be considered costume pieces and will be handled by the costume designer depending on the theater and the item. Similarly, depending on the production and the items, set dressing may fall to the scenic designer. If it is uncertain whether something falls under the "prop" category, the "costume" category, or the "scenic" category, make note of it and address it during a production meeting. Establish early on who will be responsible for obtaining that item and whose budget it will fall under. Stay on top of these items. If a particular team isn't given responsibility for the item, it will likely fall through the cracks or be forgotten about until the last minute. If it falls to multiple teams, remind both parties of it often and make sure it is being addressed.

Pay particular attention to the props in the show. Typically, these are the aspect of the script that will be changed the most to fit each particular production. Since most of these changes are decided in rehearsals, the stage manager will need to keep careful track of them and make sure they are all clearly communicated to the props master. The stage manager may also have a hand in dealing with props, as they are often responsible for obtaining and keeping track of rehearsal props as well as tracking the props as they move around and onstage/offstage during the show. For these reasons, it can be beneficial to maintain a personal props list, separate from the master list maintained by the props master. Schedule regular check-ins with them throughout the process to confirm that both lists are accurate and up to date (see Appendix A.1).

After the preliminary prop lists are made, it is important to go over them with the director (who may have a list of their own). Sometimes they can tell you right away whether they are planning to use something or not.

Expendables

Make note of perishable props that will require multiples throughout the run. Always insure that there will be extras; if the text calls for one shattered vase, make sure that there are enough extras for all performances, as well as rehearsals and accidents.

Some examples of expendables are:

- Paper that will be written on/ripped up/crumpled;
- Edibles and drinks;
- Breakables (not everything that could break, but things intentionally broken or disfigured during each performance, e.g., vases that need to be shattered or clocks that need to be smashed).

In some scripts, there will be a props list provided at the end of the text. Just as with the stage directions, this is a list that has usually been compiled by the stage manager of a particular production. This means that, while it can provide a good starting place for your list, it should by no means be relied upon to be complete or correct for the script. It may skip some props or add some according to the needs of that particular production. As such, always make and maintain your own list based on the text.

Scenic Breakdowns

The next piece of paperwork you need to complete is a scenic breakdown. A scenic breakdown outlines each Act and Scene as it is divided in the script and details which pages it is on, the locale of the scene (if indicated), which characters are onstage (or speaking/singing offstage), and a short description of the action. For musicals, it also details which musical numbers are in each scene. This step will assist in the scheduling of rehearsals (for easy identification of who needs to be called for each scene). It also gives you a simplified visual breakdown of the play to help keep things straight while you are still familiarizing yourself with it (see Appendix B).

Depending on the script and on your rehearsal needs, you may find it useful to make a French scene breakdown. French scenes are delineated by any entrance/exit of an actor (there may be multiple French scenes in a single book scene). This type of breakdown is useful for plays that are not broken down into acts and scenes (see Appendix B.1).

Once complete, share the production analysis and scenic breakdown with the rest of the production team. This will give them a good starting place, as well as an opportunity for everyone to compare notes and make sure that no design elements are overlooked.

Basic Tools and Supplies

There are basic tools and supplies that all stage managers should invest in. Listed below are a few of the more critical ones. For a complete list, see Stage Management Kit (p. 50).

Office Supplies

A good stage manager is never without a full stock of office supplies. From pens, pencils, and highlighters to paper, sticky notes, a hole punch, and a stapler, all will become critical to have on hand. Invest in high-quality supplies for your own use, as well as cheaper extras of everything to provide for your team. Inevitably, the actors will forget a pencil, the director will forget notepaper, and no one will ever have an eraser. Usually, the stage manager can (and should) be reimbursed for shared office supplies, so be sure to keep receipts for these purchases.

> Back-to-school season is a great time to stock up on office supplies.

Tape

As a stage manager many different types of tape are required for different purposes and jobs. Gaffers (gaff) tape, spike tape, glow tape, and Marley tape will be the four most heavily used tapes. These are often available from the venue and are kept in a secured storage location when not in use. If not, they will likely be purchased out of the stage management budget.

> It is a good idea to invest a little money into a personal tape stock, but be careful to get reimbursed for the tape you use, as it gets expensive quickly. One roll of gaff tape and a couple colors of spike tape are a good starting place; glow tape and Marley tape are good additional items to have around.

Tools

Similarly to office supplies, there are a few standard tools that a stage manager should invest in. These include a high-quality 30-foot tape measure, a flat reel cloth or metal tape measure, a screwdriver (with both Phillips and flathead options), a utility knife, a stopwatch, and an architect's scale ruler. Also highly recommended are a multi tool, a hex key set, and a power strip.

Scripts

Scripts will typically come from the director, artistic director, production manager, company manager, or technical director. For some productions, especially musicals, the scripts and scores are rented and must be returned; for other shows, the actors may keep the scripts. You should ascertain what will happen to the scripts at the end of the production. If they are to be returned, make sure the date of return is clear. If scripts must be returned, number each script or score in pencil and have the actors sign them out in order to keep track of which actor has which script (this sign-out sheet can also double as a damage waiver with a few added sentences) (see Appendix C). Keep a list of this information in your promptbook and a secondary copy with the packing list provided in the shipment of the scripts. Additionally, remind actors (and musicians, when applicable) that only light pencil marks are allowed on all rented scripts/scores and all marks MUST be erased before return. It is your responsibility to double-check that all scripts/scores have been erased once returned and prior to shipping. Whenever possible, keep an extra copy of the script in your stage manager's kit for when a new team member suddenly comes on-board or when an actor forgets his script. Make sure this script is kept updated with all script changes if any occur.

Even if the company does not have a damage policy, the suggestion of a fine usually tends to keep people more honest.

Online Resources

There are a number of online resources that you can utilize for your production. These can make sharing documents, calendars, scripts, etc. much easier. Check with the theater to see what resources they already have in place or are used and begin there. Here are a few commonly used options.

Cloud-Based Storage

An online resource that stores all data in the cloud, allowing everyone on the team shared access from all of their devices. If the company isn't already using some sort of cloud storage, it would be a good idea to set it up, as it makes communication and collaboration much easier. There are numerous companies that offer cloud-based storage, so explore the options to find which works best for you and the company. Below are two that have been used with great success.

It is important to remember to copy things from Dropbox, not drag and drop. Files on Dropbox don't automatically duplicate like with other programs. If a file is dragged out of Dropbox onto a user's computer, it is removed from Dropbox entirely. Remind the others shared on the folder as well.

Dropbox

A Dropbox can be created for every production so that research, ideas, paperwork, and reports can be shared and easily accessed by all members of the production team. The size limitation of the free accounts can be prohibitive for storing multiple large files.

Google Docs

An alternative to Dropbox is Google Drive. If your team primarily uses Gmail, this can be a very easy way to share documents that can be accessed anywhere with Internet. Some nice things about Google Drive is that the space is unlimited if the documents are created using the program, you can easily see when other people have edited the document, and you can also simultaneously edit a document with other users and see their progress. You can also customize how much or how little each person can interact with the document (from full editing capabilities to just reading), to avoid accidental changes.

Calendars

Ensuring that everyone in the process is working from the same schedule and keeping it updated typically falls to the stage manager. Having an easily updatable and accessible calendar will save time and energy for the entire team. Posting the rehearsal schedule on this calendar is a great way to make sure everyone has access to the information without having to constantly contact you.

Google Calendar

Google Calendar is a great tool for creating a rehearsal and production calendar. Google calendars can be easily shared with the production staff and actors and are easy to access and sync from mobile devices, as well as interfacing well with most desktop calendar programs.

Microsoft Exchange

If the theater utilizes a Microsoft Exchange system, the calendar within Microsoft Outlook also works well, but it doesn't always play as well with other platforms so use with care.

Scheduling Resources

Scheduling is a huge part of the stage manager's job, and any tools to help wrangle everyone's schedule will make your life easier and more productive.

Meeting Wizard

www.meetingwizard.com is a great way to find open times in team members' schedules, and send meeting reminders.

Doodle

www.doodle.com is another option similar to Meeting Wizard and easily allows for finding open time in all team members' schedules.

Other Resources

Google Sites/Wikispaces

Google Sites and Wikispaces are both great places to create an online callboard. These can also provide an easily accessible place for pages that have important information.

Chapter Three
The Theater

After becoming familiar with the script, it is time to get to know the theater staff, the other members of the production company, and, of course, the theater itself. This is an important time in the production process. This is time for first impressions as well as the time to find out whom you will be working with, what you will be responsible for, and where it all is. This is a great time to ask questions, find out how things have been done in the past, and any expectations for the future or new paths to explore.

Theater Staff

Every theater has a different number and type of staff. A few basic positions are listed below, but remember that titles and duties vary slightly from place to place and theater to theater. Some members of the theater staff are also members of the production artistic staff. Many smaller theaters may have one person in multiple roles. In Figure 3.1 we introduce several of the positions that a stage manager is most likely to interact with; it is, as you can tell from the diagram, not a comprehensive list.

Producer

Producers manage the overall financial functions of a theatrical organization, they hire and fire, sign paychecks, and typically have final say over all decisions. Producers frequently also have a large hand in season selection. Remember during all interactions with the producer that continued and future employment depend a lot on how you present yourself, how you handle the production process, and your overall attitude.

Artistic Director (AD)

Artistic directors maintain the artistic vision of the theatre company and production as a whole. Often artistic directors direct productions, but when they are not directing they will act as a resource for directors and the artistic staff. For companies that do not have a producer, the artistic director will typically fill many of the producer's roles.

Production Manager (PM)

Production managers are responsible for the implementation and realization of the creative team's artistic vision. The production manager typically acts as the liaison between the artistic staff and the director and will work hand in hand with the stage manager to insure that the rehearsal process and production process flow smoothly.

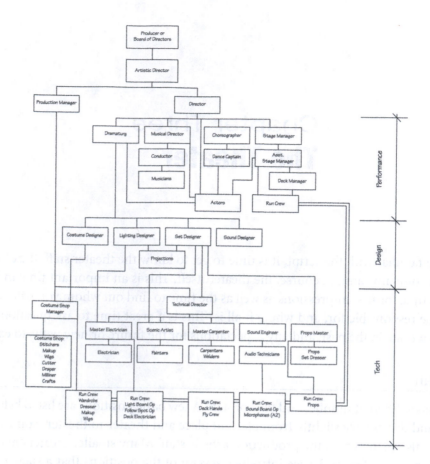

Figure 3.1 Diagram of Theatrical Hierarchy

Technical Director (TD)

The technical director supervises and/or implements all technical aspects of a production. They are also, typically, in charge of the scene shop and all scenic construction as well as scenic load-ins and strikes. Many will act as the liaison between the stage manager and artistic staff if a production manager is not present within the company.

Costume Shop Supervisor/Manager

Costume shop supervisors/managers run the costume shop, building and/or pulling costumes to realize the costume designer's vision. This position works closely with the stage manager to schedule fittings and provide rehearsal costumes (shoes, skirts, corsets, etc.).

Scene Shop Supervisor

Larger theaters have bigger staffs and there may be someone who is dedicated to supervising the day-to-day goings-on of the scene shop. This person may be able to keep you informed on the progress of the build and pieces needed for rehearsal or be a conduit to communicate more easily with the shop.

Director

The director oversees the production. They provide the artistic vision that guides the designers and actors to create the world of the play. The stage manager works most directly with this individual and it is their job to partner with the director to insure the team follows the director's vision.

Design Team

The team of designers creates the visual and aural world of the play; this process uses many different mediums, starting with visual and aural research, moving on to sketching, drawing, drafting, computer-aided drafting, rendering, and models, finally culminating in a realized design. Sometimes a single designer will perform multiple roles, other times only one. Communication with all members of the artistic staff is extremely important. All people involved in the process are busy and have feelings. Many designers tend to be very precious about their time and designs; phrasing a question in the wrong way can easily ruffle feathers, and getting to know the different personalities quickly will save many headaches down the road. Depending on the size of the theater, there may be associate and assistant designers as well. Associate designers are the designer's right hand; they typically are heavily involved in the design process and can make executive decisions if the designer isn't present. Assistant designers assist both the designer and associate designer. They interface with the shops and staff a lot, run errands, and deal with paperwork. Typically they cannot make final decisions without the designer's approval.

Scenographer

A scenographer designs all elements of the production, creating a more holistic design. Instead of a design team consisting of individual designers, a single person creates the entire visual and aural world of the play. While uncommon in the United States, scenographers are still prevalent in Europe.

Scenic Designer

The scenic designer creates the visual world of the scenery (set), i.e., what the world surrounding the actors looks like (from an empty stage to the grand palace of the King of Siam). The scenic design heavily influences the blocking patterns of the production (where the furniture sits, where the doors and pathways are located, etc.). It is important to communicate with the designer constantly throughout the rehearsal periods as things are "discovered" in rehearsal and modifications need to be made. Small modifications such as furniture placement can happen throughout the process. However, large modifications cannot be made after the shop has begun the build process, so make sure the designer and director are communicating openly and clearly and speaking the same language (this will make your life easier down the road). The scenic designer is responsible for creating groundplans, elevations, renderings, and models. Always insure you are working with the most current drawings in rehearsal. It will adversely affect the process if the director and stage manager are working off of out-of-date drawings.

Costume Designer

The costume designer creates the visual world of the costumes, i.e., what each actor wears (clothing, jewelry, shoes, etc.). Just as with the scenic designer, what the costume designer chooses to dress the actors in will influence their movement around the stage. For example, if it is a period piece, the large skirts need to be taken into account in large group scenes. If an actress is in five-inch heels, they probably cannot run up stairs or perform really involved choreography, especially if they aren't the most graceful, which is a helpful thing to figure out. The costume designer can also play a vital role in helping the actors discover and embody their characters by putting them literally and emotionally "in the shoes" of their character.

The costume designer is responsible for creating a costume plot, piece list (itemized list of all costume pieces), and renderings of the costumes. Depending on the show, there may also be a makeup and/or hair/wig designer, separate from the costume designer. This is common on period pieces or fantastical shows requiring specialized makeup and hair.

Properties (Props) Master/Designer

The props master/designer creates, buys, and/or finds hand props and set dressing to round out the world being created. They must coordinate closely with the other departments and designers to make sure that the props align with the cohesive vision of the production. It is important to communicate clearly and frequently with the props master/designer—they need to know how things are being handled, what additions have been made since the original lists were created, and any other pertinent information (the chair needs to be strong enough to stand on, the hairbrush should be blue, etc.).

Lighting Designer

The lighting designer lights the visual world created by the scenic and costume designers. They also add to and create parts of the visual world. Lighting designers are typically more in the background of the design process at the start, as much of their work is dependent on the other designers. However, it is important to keep them communicating with the other designers so there are no surprises for anyone further down the line. Lighting designers are responsible for creating the lightplot, selecting gel colors and gobos, and creating a cue list notating placement of lighting cues.

Sound Designer

The sound designer creates the aural world of the play (what the audience hears), whether that is the quiet ambience of a river in the distance or gunshots and car crashes. The sound designer is responsible for creating a sound cue list notating the placement of the sound cues. Sometimes the designer will also be responsible for creating and/or providing rehearsal sound cues.

Projection Designer

Just like every other designer in the process they are responsible for creating and designing the content that will be seen on the projection surface(s). A relatively newer field, projections are quickly gaining traction as an "easy, inexpensive" way to create scenery and locations. This is not to undercut the position of projection designer. The projection designer should furnish a cue list to the stage manager prior to technical (tech) rehearsals.

Music Director

Music directors work with the director to shape the music of a production. They can help make decisions about cuts in a dance break or adding a few measures to a vamp. Sometimes the music director assists with the casting process, lending advice about vocal ability to help the director make final decisions. They will teach the cast the music and, typically, play for the rehearsals. In some companies the music director helps find and engage the pit musicians. They are responsible for the technical singing and orchestral portions of a musical, and often are the orchestra conductor as well.

Choreographer

The choreographer creates the dances and movement patterns of the actors during musical numbers. Choreographers and directors work very closely during musicals and it is important that the rest of the design team understands the needs of the dance pieces (dancing on furniture, doing splits, etc.) so the costumes and set pieces can function as needed with the choreography. Depending on the director's skill set, the director may also act as the choreographer.

Fight Choreographer

If the show includes any fight or battle sequences (both armed and unarmed combat), a fight choreographer may also be hired to insure the safety of all participants in the fight. Depending on the extent of the fight(s), the fight choreographer may only be present for a few rehearsals. Before leaving the production, they will assign a member of the cast to be the fight captain. This individual is charged with maintaining the integrity of the fights and, above all, insuring that they are being performed safely.

Other Staff Members

Assistant Stage Managers (ASM)

Depending on the company you may have assistants through the entire process, once you have started runs, or not until tech rehearsals start. Frequently the assistant stage manager is in charge of the deck (stage). It is important to have a good working relationship with your assistant stage managers because they will often be your link to what is happening backstage and your representative to the cast and crew.

Accompanist/Rehearsal Pianist

If the music director isn't playing during auditions or rehearsals, an accompanist or a rehearsal pianist is used. It is important to take them into account when scheduling rehearsals and keep them in the loop about any scheduling updates. Whenever possible, let them know what will be worked on each day as well. This is a nice gesture and will allow them to better prepare for rehearsal.

Crew (Deck Crew/Fly Crew/Wardrobe Crew/Board and Spot Operators)

The crew work behind the scenes during tech week and for the run of the production to help create a seamless, smooth, and consistent show night after night.

The deck crew (also called "run crew") work backstage, moving set pieces, setting props, pulling curtains, and anything else that must be done to make the set function. The assistant stage manager or the deck chief is responsible for running this team.

The fly crew are responsible for the operation of all flylines, which move the flying scenery in and out of position for each scene. One of the harder and more precise jobs, it requires crew members to move large, heavy pieces of scenery into place at a very specific time in order to avoid hitting cast and crew members maneuvering around during a scene change. Theatre is the only industry in the world that allows people to pass under large, heavy objects while they are in motion; as such it is very important everyone knows their job and proper safety procedures.

The wardrobe crew also work backstage, although typically they are in the dressing rooms, rather than in the wings. The wardrobe crew are responsible for helping with costume, hair, and makeup changes. They are also typically responsible for maintenance of the dressing rooms, as well as laundry duty. These crew usually work closely with the wardrobe supervisor.

Board operators run the lightboard and the soundboard. If the production calls for projections, sometimes a separate individual is hired to run this as well. These crew members work with the staff and/or designers to learn how to run the board, how to run system checks, and basic troubleshooting techniques should anything go wrong. Soundboard operators run mics as well as sound cues. Depending on the theater, they may be stationed in the house rather than the booth for acoustic purposes.

Spot operators run the spotlights. They work directly with the lighting designer to learn their cues and spot techniques.

The stage manager is responsible for calling out all board cues during the show. As such, they will be in direct contact with each of these operators, over headset, via cue light, or in the booth. Depending on the production, experience of the spot operators, and the complexity of the spot cues, the stage manager may call spot cues as well.

The theatrical community is a small close-knit community; everybody knows everyone else and word travels fast. Never burn bridges and always remember that a reputation, good or bad, will follow you around. You may have never heard of the person you are talking to at a new theater, but that doesn't mean they have not heard of you, or the places you have previously worked and the work you have done.

Dramaturge

Dramaturges provide information about the script, time period, writer, and anything else relevant to the production. They may provide a glossary if there are a lot of unusual words or find articles that give context to an aspect of the setting of the play.

Get In Their Shoes

This job entails interaction with and coordination of all of the aforementioned positions. In order to better connect and sympathize with each of these team members, try your hand at as many of them as you can! Take a course in directing and acting. Ask to attend a fittings session with the costume designer and wardrobe manager. Take a break from stage managing and ask instead to assist with lights or sound. Get on your work gear and spend a Saturday in the scene shop building. Shadow the choreographer or music director in a class or workshop. Many of these people will love to share their knowledge with you and will appreciate that you take an interest in their passion! More than that, it will give you invaluable insight into what their work is like, allow you to learn the terminology, and better equip you to coordinate schedules, anticipate issues between departments, and truly be the connecting fiber for the whole production team.

First Meeting with the Director

This is a very important step in the process, as it is the stage manager's primary job to communicate the ideas of the director clearly to everyone else in the process and make sure everyone is on the same page. Plan this meeting as early as possible. Communication between the two of you will be much easier once this first meeting has occurred and you will be much more effective in your work once you know how the whole process is going to work.

Discussion Points

- What does the director expect from you?
  - How do they prefer to be addressed (first name, last name, nickname, sir/ma'am)?
  - What is the best way to reach him/her (e-mail, cell/office/home phone, call vs. text, face-to-face meetings)?
  - When is it acceptable to do so (no calls after 9 p.m., e-mail only during work hours, etc.)?
  - What role should you play in the rehearsal room? (Do they want or expect input from you or the room (cast)? Do they want you to start/end rehearsals? Are you expected/allowed to give notes? Should you give corrections during scene work or after?)
  - Do they want to start immediately on time or have a couple of minutes of friendly chat at the top of the day?
- Who will be making the rehearsal schedule? (Will it be made after the day's rehearsal for the next day? Will it be made a week at a time? Does the director have a schedule for the entire process? How much should be sent to the actors? Will the director give you a list of things that they want to work and let you figure out when they fit into the day or do they want to work chronologically? Will rehearsals be split? Do they want to announce an off-book (line memorization) date?)
- Who will be running production meetings (depending on the theater, this may be decided by or up to the producer, artistic director, production manager, or technical director)?
- When would they like to start using rehearsal props? (Day one, after initial blocking, or once scripts are out of hands? Are there certain pieces that need to be the final prop?)
- When and how often do they want to build in breaks during rehearsal?
  - Many companies use the AEA standard breaks (a ten-minute break after every eighty minutes of rehearsal or a five-minute break after fifty-five minutes of rehearsal), although some directors will want to break after a section is complete.
  - How would they like you to get their attention when it's time for a break (slide them a note, stand up, give a two-minute warning, etc.)?
  - When coming back from a break will they start immediately or need a minute to get back on track?
- Do they have any pet peeves (breaking mid-moment, actors that aren't in the scene entering/exiting the rehearsal space, gum chewing, actors not wearing closed-toed shoes)?

- Discuss the director's concept.
  - Have an in-depth discussion about the play. Make sure to discuss the plot, concept, and specific needs of this production. (For this reason, it is crucial that you come into this meeting having read the play and with an understanding of the characters.) Take notes.
  - Make sure you have an in-depth understanding of the director's vision of the world of the play. Once the show opens, it will be your responsibility to maintain the artistic integrity of the show as envisioned by the director, so a clear understanding of their vision and concept is critical.
    - Academic productions typically differ in this respect because the director is usually present during the entire show process, so the stage manager may not be responsible for maintaining the integrity of the show.
- Discuss the design/production team and the role they will play with the specific production and company.
  - All designers, choreographers, music directors, technical director, etc.
  - This is also the time to discuss any assistant stage managers. Determine if you will have any and, if so, who is in charge of hiring them (stage manager, production manager, artistic director) and what their responsibilities will be for this particular production.
- Determine rules for rehearsals and the company.
  - Food and drink policies, noise and guests, sign-in procedures, emergency procedures, late policies, etc.
- Discuss what you expect from the director.
  - What is the best method for them to communicate with you (e-mail, cell/office/home phone, texting, etc.)?
- Establish a plan to meet briefly after every rehearsal. This is a good, consistent time when you will both be available to check in about the process and to discuss any issues or questions that arose during rehearsal. Daily communication is key to a successful director/stage manager working relationship (if post-rehearsal meetings are too difficult, find a time when you can both check in).

Remember that directors and stage managers are co-workers and team members (even in an educational environment). Don't be demanding, but know that you deserve respect. If you both make your expectations clear up front, there is less likely to be a major blow-up later in the process.

Tour of the Theater

Early in the process, request a tour of the theater. This will likely be conducted by either your technical director or the venue manager. You will be given a great deal of information on this tour, so it is in your best interest to take notes as you go. Here are some questions you may want to ask or make sure are addressed on your tour:

- Where is the rehearsal space?
- Is there a callboard? If so, where?
- Is there a separate stage manager/administration room/office?
- What is the protocol for locking up the theater? Which doors need to be locked, what lights need to be double-checked, etc.?
  - If there is security personnel, gather their contact information. Meet them in person, if possible.

- Does the theater have its own house manager and front of house staff? If so, gather the relevant contact information and meet them in person, if possible.
- How do you communicate backstage? Is there a headset or intercom system setup available? If not, how have past users of the space solved this issue?
- Are there monitors (broadcast an audio and/or video feed from the stage) backstage or in the green room and dressing rooms?
- Where are the controls for the work lights and the house lights?
- Are there any phones or alarms that need to be turned off or disabled during performances?
- What is the policy for theatrical smoke and haze?
- What is the policy on smoking or open flame onstage?
- What is the policy on the use of weapons onstage? Is there somewhere to lock the weapons away securely?
- What is the policy on food and drinks in the house? In the dressing room? In the green room?
- Locate walk-throughs and cross-overs (paths that actors can take backstage to get from stage right to stage left without being seen by the audience). In some rare cases this might be outside, which presents another set of challenges to work through.
- Heat/AC control? Is that the stage manager's job or is the venue responsible for adjusting?
- Is there a back of house calling position or is the stage manager's station backstage?
- Are any of the spaces shared? Off limits? What does this mean in regards to the rehearsal and production process? Are there "quiet" hours?
- What are the emergency procedures and policies? What is the venue's policy regarding fire proofing?
- What are the parking policies? Are there specific lots/spots reserved for patrons only?
- Is there Wi-Fi available? What is the code, if necessary?

Rooms and Important Features

The Stage

This will be the main playing space for the show. As the stage manager, take the time to become as intimately familiar with it as possible. Learn where the floor squeaks or is uneven, how to keep it clean (the best mopping and sweeping patterns to get the most dust, where to vacuum), where the best backstage hiding spots are for props and actors, sightlines for the audience, the quirks of the curtains, what doors squeak or slam, and anything else that may help, impede, or otherwise impact the production. The more you know, the better the production can be shaped to best fit in the space.

Scene Shop

Depending on the layout and size of the theater, the scene shop may be an important part of the rehearsal or production process, whether it acts as a rehearsal space during the rehearsal period or storage and a pass-through during production. Determine the need and usage of the space to plan for time and staff to clean, clear, and maintain the scene shop as needed relating to rehearsal and performance. Some scene shops are located off-site. In this case, transportation of the scenery to the theater for load-in will have to be coordinated. This usually falls to the technical director or the production manager to handle, but is good to take into consideration.

Costume Shop

Depending on the layout and size of the theater, the costume shop may be an important part of the production process. It may act as dressing room space or wardrobe space, and typically houses the laundry facilities and supplies that will be used to perform costume maintenance during the run of a performance. If the costume shop is used as a dressing room space, determine what steps must be taken to keep the shop in working order during non-production times.

Dressing Rooms

It is important that the dressing rooms are kept neat and orderly throughout the entire production process. While it is the actor's personal space, it still needs to be kept clean and usable. Typically, (depending on the theater's policies) no food or drink should be allowed in dressing rooms or anywhere near costumes (water in a closed-lidded bottle is acceptable). Find out if dressing room maintenance is the stage manager's responsibility or if it falls to the wardrobe crew (if one exists).

Booth (Control Room)

This is the room or place in the theater where the lightboard and soundboard are located. In many theaters, the booth is where the stage manager will be stationed during shows to call cues and oversee the performance. This area may also house the theatrical systems for the theater (dimmer racks, amplifier racks, control computers, etc.). This is typically one of the more secure areas of the theater because of the amount of equipment contained in it. Occasionally, there will instead be a podium or station backstage, sometimes referred to as the prompt corner. This often includes a desk (prompt desk) and a monitor, as audio and video are important to allow the stage manager to see and hear the cue lines. Determine who has keys to this room/area and how it is secured.

The Callboard

The callboard is where the company goes for important information regarding the production. It is often a corkboard or similar bulletin board and is placed in a centralized location easily accessible in the theater. Common places are in the green room or right inside the stage door. The callboard should include a daily sign-in sheet, the rehearsal calendar, the daily/weekly rehearsal schedule, fittings schedules, and important notifications or announcements. In professional union productions, this will also include some paperwork as required by the Actors' Equity Association. Keep the information on this callboard up to date and consistent with any information distributed electronically or verbally. Actors can be forgetful and this gives them a place to check for correct information without always having to ask their stage manager first hand. If a board doesn't already exist, scout out the best place for one and plan extra time and materials to make one before load-into the theater.

Rehearsal Space

In many cases, the performance space will not be available to use until tech week, so rehearsals will take place in a secondary location. Just as with the theater, you will be responsible for preparing and maintaining this space. Once rehearsals are moved to the performance space, be sure to leave the rehearsal space in a clean, usable condition for the next production. This includes removing ("pulling") spike tape, sweeping and mopping, emptying trash, etc.

If the rehearsal space is rented or used by multiple productions or classes, check with the staff or renter to dictate appropriate use of the space, as well as how the space needs to be left at the end of each rehearsal. Follow these rules carefully and maintain a strong and positive relationship with the owners and fellow users of the space. Doing so is not only courteous, but will also increase the likelihood of being invited back for future productions and being granted some favors (such as storage space for props, ability to leave tape on the floor, use of in-house props/ furniture, etc.). Remember to treat rented spaces just like you would treat your own personal space (or better); many of these rentals have security deposits just like apartments and even small things may cost the company money.

> Remember, pulling up spike tape can pull up the floor finish underneath, so always check and make sure the tape will not damage the floor before putting it down.

Prop and Costume Storage

Most theaters have a storage area or facilities where costumes, set pieces, furniture, and hand props are stored. This is where rehearsal props, costumes, and furniture can be pulled. It is important to ascertain whose responsibility that will be and the proper procedure to get access and check things out as required by the theater staff. In many cases this facility is off-site and arrangements for access or transportation of things may need to be made. Plan ahead for this.

Keys

Typically stage managers will be assigned a ring of keys or a key card to allow access to all necessary spaces. In most places it will be the stage manager's responsibility to make sure that all spaces are closed and locked once the last person leaves the building. Determine whose responsibility it will be to lock up and what needs to be done to shut down after rehearsal (turn lights off, lock access doors, shut down light and sound systems, etc.). Security is high priority, so keep careful track of keys and be diligent about checking all doors when locking up for the night. Of the production staff, the stage manager is typically the first in and the last out. If the building has additional security staff it is important to meet them and introduce yourself, since you will often be there early and late. Occasionally, when the venue is rented, the stage manager will not be issued keys. In these cases, the venue's house manager is typically responsible for unlocking and locking the building. If so, introduce yourself to these individuals and be sure to have their contact information. Keep them informed of the schedule and confirm what time you need the venue to be unlocked each day.

Cleaning Supplies

General maintenance of the space also falls under the stage manager's job description in many theaters. This primarily includes sweeping and mopping the stage, as well as keeping the theater neat during the rehearsal and performance period. As such, be sure to locate brooms, dustpans, mops, vacuums, trash-cans, and utility sinks. Find out the location and accessibility of dumpsters. If renting a space, determine whether you (the theatre company) or the venue will be responsible for providing supplies such as trash bags, bathroom items (soap, paper products), etc.

Chapter Four
Safety

Safety is the most important factor in any production. As such, it should be the top priority for the stage manager to know all safety procedures for the space, and the location of all first aid kits, fire extinguishers, emergency exits, and AED equipment (if applicable). It is also important to know the emergency protocol and safety locations of the venue. Remember, in this day and age, all decisions will eventually have to stand up to scrutiny and possible legal repercussions after the event is all said and done.

First Aid Kits

Note where all first aid kits are located; find out who is responsible for their upkeep and supply level (it might be the stage manager) and be sure they stay up to date in case of an emergency.

It is important to note any and all injuries that warrant first aid on the rehearsal or performance report—use your best judgment (e.g., a paper cut doesn't need to be noted).

Weaponry

Any shows requiring weaponry will require their own set of safety steps. All weapons will need to be locked away in a secure area whenever they are not in use. Typically, they are given their own box, crate, or carrying case that can be locked. Keys are given only to the stage manager and sometimes the fight choreographer/fight captain. Any real weapons must be made actor safe (dulled blades). Anyone using functioning firearms _must_ be given safety training and follow proper protocol in regards to the loading, unloading, and handling of these. All safety steps in regards to weaponry must be taken very seriously and enforced among the company.

Emergency Procedures

In the event of an emergency, it is important to stay calm. The stage manager is setting an example for all others to follow and if they are in a panic, others will panic too. Stage managers must use their best judgment in the event of an emergency, but always err on the side of caution. The first meeting with the theater staff is a great time to ask about the company's emergency procedures.

- Is there a designated tornado shelter area? Is it the theater? If so, what does that mean during a performance?
- Will you or the house manager be responsible for the audience in the case of an evacuation?
  - If you are responsible, arrange to get a house count for each performance as soon as one is available.
- Is there a policy in place for power outages?
  - How long do you hold the show?
  - What is the "rain check" ticketing policy?
  - Is there emergency power?
  - If you are working in an outdoor theater, do you hold at the first sign of rain or push through until you see lightning or the stage becomes unsafe?
  - If you have to hold, how long do you wait before canceling the rest of the performance?
- What is the procedure if a company member becomes ill during a performance?
- Is there a procedure in place for an armed gunman on the premises or bomb threats?
- Is there a security force associated with the theater or performance space? (This may become clear without asking—if there is security, these are good people to know.)

Some good general practices are outlined below, but remember to always use your judgment, as each situation will be unique.

Medical Emergency

Contact 9-1-1 if you feel emergency personnel are warranted. In conjunction with the house manager, attempt to quietly and calmly remove the person in question to the lobby without disturbing the production to allow emergency personnel easy access and keep the audience calm. If necessary, make an announcement to hold the show and inform the audience calmly what is taking place and that the show will continue when possible. If working in an academic setting, contact Campus Security to inform them of the situation as well; depending on the campus there may be varying protocols for contacting security. If working in an arts center environment, contact Building Security if applicable. While many companies and theaters request that local security (academic, building) be contacted first, this can delay the response time of emergency personnel, so it is best to make a judgment call in these situations that will best serve the person having the emergency.

Security Emergency

Contact 9-1-1 (or, if applicable, Campus or Building Security) if you feel emergency personnel are warranted. If needed, calmly direct patrons to the safest location for the situation.

Weather

Remain calm, use the house address system (if applicable) to inform patrons of the issue, and follow the procedure discussed in the first meeting with the theater staff. In the case of weather events (tornados, flooding, etc.), find out the safest place for patrons.

Suspicious Persons

If possible lock the theater doors to keep the person or persons out. Wait for emergency personnel for additional instructions.

Fire

Contact 9-1-1, make an announcement to the audience, and direct them to quickly and calmly move to the nearest emergency exit. To the best of your ability try to account for all of the people in the theater (cast, crew, audience) once it has been evacuated.

Injury Report

If ever a member of the team is injured during rehearsals, workdays, or performances, an injury report should be filled out (or at least be available and offered). This documents the name of the injured, the date, the circumstances and severity of the injury, and any necessary follow-up (ambulance called, doctor's visit required, etc.).

If considering pursuing stage management as a career or a lifelong hobby, take a course in first aid and get CPR, AED, and Bloodborne Pathogen Certified. This is often required of professional stage managers and will serve you extremely well when faced with the inevitable injuries that occur backstage, onstage, or in the rehearsal space.

Chapter Five
Auditions

Before Auditions

The stage manager's role in the audition process will vary depending on the production and the theatre company. Sometimes, producers and artistic directors like to personally set up and take care of many of the details for auditions. It is important to determine who makes these decisions and arrangements. Remember that every audition process is unique.

Meet with the Producer, Artistic Director, and Director

Communication is paramount to every step of the production process. Once you determine who is responsible for making the decisions about auditions, schedule a meeting with the appropriate people to find out details of the audition and callback days (dates, times, location, schedule, dance call). If there is a dance call, check in with the choreographer about their needs prior to the call.

During these meetings find out what the auditionees will need to prepare. Will it be a cold reading? Will they need to prepare specific materials? Get a detailed list of the sides needed for the auditions, if sides will be required. If it is a musical, what music will they need to prepare? Will they need to demonstrate any other talents (dance, choreography, etc.)? Will nudity be required, or appearance alterations (hair cut, style, color, etc.)?

Determine who will be responsible for sending out audition announcements: will the stage manager be coordinating the audition announcements and fielding questions, or will the company be taking care of this?

This is also the time to ask any other questions you may have about auditions, equipment, or personnel needs. For musicals, do you need to find an accompanist for music auditions? A piano? Sound equipment to play musical tracks? Where are auditions taking place and who is responsible for reserving the space? Will the director be reading individuals, groups, or pairs? Should the auditionees stay after their initial read? Will the dance call be on the same day in the same place? Are you responsible for setting up the room (tables, keyboards, etc.)? Does the director want you in the room or will you be coordinating the auditionees?

Prep Audition Material

If the stage manager is responsible for audition announcements, it may fall to them to make announcement posters, Web listings, or advertisements. Sign-up sheets, audition information forms, a character breakdown, and sides may also be required.

Audition Form

Audition forms should include legal name, stage name, phone numbers, preferred e-mail address, height, weight, hair color, age range, vocal range, previous experience, special skills, and scheduling conflicts. Some theaters require a headshot to be attached as well (see Appendix D).

- Include a note about makeup kits and shoes. Depending on the theater, actors will be required to provide their own makeup and/or character shoes.
- Check with the director at your audition meeting to determine any additional information or questions they may want to include.

Character Breakdown

Character breakdowns provide basic information regarding the characters in the show: name, relationship to other characters in the play, age, and brief description. This information is often provided within the script or available from the publisher. Auditionees can use this information to decide which roles they want to audition for or to gain insight into the relationships in the sides they are reading (see Appendix E).

Sides

Sides are scenes selected from the play to be used as audition material. These scenes should be chosen (by the director) at the audition meeting so you can make copies and have them available with the sign-up sheets and audition forms. These copies should be neat and easy to read so that auditions can run smoothly. Always print a few more than you think you will need.

Preliminary Schedule

This should outline the general rehearsal period, tech week (i.e., required rehearsals), and performance dates. This will allow the actors to plan around the rehearsal period and not be surprised by required production dates. This will also give them a chance to report any already known conflicts to you so that the rehearsal schedule can be made accordingly. Provide a place on the audition sheet for auditionees to list any known conflicts.

Make it clear that conflicts listed on the conflict sheet will be worked around as much as possible. Any conflicts NOT written on the conflict sheet may not be accounted for and the person will not be excused from rehearsal regardless of the conflict. Exceptions to this can be decided on a case-by-case basis at the discretion of the director. **Always note that attendance of all rehearsals and performances from tech through strike are required for all actors, crew, and stage management.**

At Auditions

The process will be long and hectic. It is important to come prepared with extra sides, pens/pencils, paper, a folder for audition sheets, blank audition sheets, clipboards, and a positive attitude. There will be little time to gather any of the items during auditions, so make sure they are easily accessible when needed.

Many times actors may read for multiple roles. Keep track of who reads what part and who reads in what groups, so later that information is available if needed to make decisions for callbacks or as a reminder of what took place during the audition process.

Staying on schedule is important, but often almost impossible. It is the stage manager's job to do their very best to keep auditions running on time. Give gentle reminders to the director when someone's time is up, but remember that it is important that the director gets the time they need with each auditionee.

> With musicals and larger productions, it may be helpful to have an assistant to keep order outside the audition room and to wrangle the auditionees. If possible, recruit a potential assistant stage manager or a friend to help.

Callbacks

After the initial culling of the herd (large group auditions are often called cattle calls), the director, choreographer, and/or music director come up with a list of people they would like to "callback" or invite to an additional, more specialized or concentrated audition. These typically take place within a few days of auditions. A callback list needs to be generated and posted on the callboard and other locations where the given theater specifically posts information.

While auditions are designed to get a feel of the talent of one individual, callbacks are typically meant to form the best ensemble from the selected talent pool. The director will likely have a list of characters that they would like each actor to read and additional sides or selections for callbacks that are different from the audition sides. These will need to be made available to the actors at callbacks. This can be when all of those notes you took about who read what and with whom will be helpful to refresh the director's memory.

Often actors will be called for the full callback time, released only when instructed by the director. The actors will be split into smaller ensemble groups and cast according to the needs of the sides, allowing each actor the chance to read for all of the roles the director is considering them for. For your sanity, it is important to keep close track of who reads for which role to make sure that no one is overlooked accidentally.

After Auditions

Sometimes it will be the responsibility of the stage manager to post the cast list. Speak with the director or artistic director to find out how cast lists are typically distributed (via e-mail, posting on a callboard, carrier pigeon). Include the date, time, and location of the first rehearsal. You may also thank everyone for their time and effort during the audition process, if you so desire.

Chapter Six
Pre-Production

Getting Organized

Once the show has been cast and the artistic team has been selected, there is some preparation that must be done before beginning the production process. Once the production is underway, things will be hectic, constantly changing, and time will slip away quickly. The best way to prepare for this inevitability is to take steps to over-prepare as much as possible before the process begins. This step, often referred to as "prep week," involves creating the promptbook, preparing paperwork, creating the rehearsal schedule, preparing the space for rehearsals, and restocking the stage manager's kit.

The Promptbook

The first step in any prep week is creating the promptbook. The promptbook, sometimes called the "Show Bible" or "The Book," is a binder containing any and all important information pertaining to the show. This binder is put together and maintained by the stage manager. Typically, this will require a rather large binder (anywhere from 2 to 5 inches depending on the show). It is best to use a view binder (the kind with a plastic sleeve around the outside), so a cover page and spine label can be used to easily identify it as the show promptbook. Use binder tabs or dividers to separate the major sections (e.g., Cast Information, Script, Rehearsal Reports, etc.).

Promptbooks will vary from production to production, but by show time will usually include the following information.

Promptbook Checklist

1) Cast Information
   a) Cast/production team contact sheet
   b) The original or copies of the audition forms
   c) Script sign-out sheet
   d) Emergency contact forms (for everyone in the rehearsal room)
   e) A copy of the company handbook, if one exists
   f) Copies of any research/dramaturgical materials handed out to the cast throughout the production

2) Schedules and Calendars
   a) Production calendar: cast—includes rehearsals, performances, costume fittings, off-book date(s), and any additional scheduled events involving the cast or crew, etc.
   b) Production calendar: production team—includes production meetings, important rehearsal dates (run-throughs, tech rehearsals, etc.), performances, and the deadlines for all design elements
   c) Rehearsal schedule—detailed breakdown of each rehearsal (usually by day or by week, depending on the production)
   d) A conflict calendar—summary of all actor conflicts
3) Script
   a) Entrance and Exit flow chart
   b) Scene/character breakdown and/or French scene breakdown
   c) Blocking symbol/shorthand key—for anyone needing to decipher your blocking notes
   d) Blocking script—including all blocking notes
   e) Calling script—a clean copy of the script with cues written in the margins (might be the same as the blocking script)
   f) Music score (if show is a musical or has any songs)
4) Props Information
   a) Complete prop list—you may also want to indicate here which props are built, bought, borrowed, etc. for reference during strike
   b) Prop preset—this indicates where all props should be placed at the top of the show
   c) Run sheet—indicates scenic shifts and costume changes (usually only quick changes or complicated ones that are relevant to the run crew). This also tracks prop movement throughout the show
5) Scenic Information
   a) groundplan—clean copy, to scale
   b) Furniture list—you may also want to indicate here which furniture was built, bought, borrowed, etc. for reference during strike
   c) Any sketches or renderings that may be relevant to a rehearsal
6) Lighting Information
   a) Information and schedules
      i) Channel hook-up, color lists, instrument schedule, light cue list, light plot
7) Sound Information
   a) Sound cue sheet (this should be provided to you by the sound designer)
   b) Mic plot (if mics are used)—this lists which actor has which mic and tracks if mics are swapped during the run of the show
   c) Speaker plot—this shows the location of all speakers and monitors in the production and relevant information for troubleshooting purposes
8) Costume Information
   a) Costume plots/piece list—breakdown of characters by scene and each item that is worn (this should be provided to you by the costume designer)
   b) Costume sketches, if available
   c) Any special instructions regarding cleaning/maintenance
9) Rehearsal Reports
   a) Print hard copies of all rehearsal reports to keep on file

10) Performance Reports
   a) Print hard copies of all performance reports
11) Production Meeting Agendas and Notes
   a) Print hard copies of all production meeting agendas and reports to keep on file

Once production begins, the promptbook should never leave the theater. In case of an unfortunate event where the stage manager cannot attend a performance (e.g., catastrophic injury), the promptbook needs to be available and organized for the replacement. The show must go on!

Paperwork

In order to keep track of the massive amounts of information that the stage manager must be responsible for, paperwork becomes one of the top priorities. When preparing for a show it is important to use your prep week to complete, partially complete, or make a template of all the paperwork needed for the production; the stage manager can save time and mental energy later in the process that will be needed for other tasks. Use the Promptbook Checklist as a reference for what paperwork you will need to create. Some templates and paperwork samples are provided in the appendices of this book. Additionally, there are many websites and other stage management books with further examples (see Suggested Readings, p. 177). Try out multiple versions and find or create the templates that work best for you.

When first starting a new production, especially when working with a new company or new individuals, it can be difficult keeping everyone's names/roles straight. Keep a small cheat-sheet on the bottom left inside corner of the promptbook that lists all actors (full name) and the characters they play. One can also list all the members of the production team. This way, there is an easy reference that can be seen at all times, no matter which page it is opened to, and there is no need to keep flipping back to the contact sheet to remember who is playing Malvolio.

After selecting templates for all of the paperwork, the next step is to customize them for the production. Each page should include not only the name of the production, but also a few other consistent pieces of information, including the stage manager and their contact information (e-mail and phone number), date, and page __ of __. Some stage managers also list the director and the name of the production company. In addition to consistent information, paperwork should use only one or two common fonts (e.g., Times New Roman, Arial) that are consistent between all documents for each show. It is fun to choose a "show font" for the show title (one that is a bit more whimsical and matches the mood and style of the production) and then a standard, legible font for the rest of the document. This will make them easily identifiable and easy to read, and will create unity among the paperwork.

Remember over the course of your career you may do shows multiple times, so noting the producing organization will help you better keep up with your archive.

It is good practice to include the date in the name of any distributed documents so that everyone is sure to be working from the same document (e.g., Grease Rehearsal Report 9.14.pdf). This is especially important with calendars/schedules, when working off the most updated information is of the utmost importance. If multiple reports are distributed on the same day, for example a two-performance day, distinguish these in some way as well (e.g., Sylvia Performance Report 2.2 matinee.pdf and Sylvia

Performance Report 2.2 evening.pdf). If it is the same report with updated or corrected information, include UPDATED or REVISED in the title.

Each type of report/paperwork needs to contain the same information, but how it is formatted and organized is really up to the stage manager and the needs of each specific production. There is no "one form fits all" that exists.

Scheduling Rehearsals

Prep week is also when the stage manager and the director will put together a rehearsal schedule for the production. Most theaters generally work on a semi-set schedule that is adjusted depending on the conflicts and the availability of the actors for a specific production (e.g., rehearsals are always 7:00 p.m.–10:00 p.m.). Bring the scene breakdown, any known conflicts, and some scrap paper. As you are scheduling, you should confirm everyone needed for a call; sometimes the director will only want to work with some of the actors in a scene (especially with musicals—confirm whether they want to work just the song, just the dance, the book scene, or the whole thing). You may also be scheduling separate vocal work, dance calls, or measurements/fittings. In many cases, these take place simultaneously with the regular rehearsal. The stage manager is often relied on to carefully arrange these rehearsals and fittings such that no actor is accidentally scheduled to be in two places at once.

It is the stage manager's job to go through the audition forms and compile all actor conflicts. It can be beneficial to create a conflict calendar rather than just a list. Bring these to the scheduling meeting and try to create a schedule around these conflicts. Make sure the actors know that, as much as possible, their conflicts will be worked around but that not all conflicts will be able to be accounted for. Include a note on the audition form that any conflicts **not** included on the conflict sheet may not be excused. Any unexpected conflicts are handled on a case-by-case basis and are usually decided upon by the director, stage manager, artistic director, and producer as needed.

If in an academic setting, remember to take the food service hours into account when scheduling rehearsals. If food is not being provided, all students on the meal plan need to be given at least a thirty-minute break during the food services operating hours to eat. In a professional environment, make sure to take any union regulations into account if applicable.

Once the rehearsal schedule is complete, distribute it to all members of the team. The production team (including the director) should be given a production calendar that includes production meetings, design deadlines, run-throughs, tech rehearsals, dress rehearsals, and performance dates. Actors, stage management, and the directors should be given a similar production calendar that includes rehearsals, costume fittings, tech rehearsals, dress rehearsals, performance dates, and any other miscellaneous events that include the cast. They should also receive daily schedules that include details on what will be rehearsed each night (scene(s), act(s), which actor(s)/character(s) are required, music/choreography/fight calls, etc.). Copies of all three of these schedules should be posted on the callboard and kept in the promptbook. Remember to keep all of these schedules updated throughout the process. Online calendars can help keep things up to date, but can also create their own set of problems so use with caution (see Appendix F, F.1).

It is important to find the balance between how much information you give out and when. It is easy for people to forget that schedules can change and it can be frustrating (and confusing) to have conflicting information sent out. On the other hand, it is important for people to know what is happening so they can plan accordingly. Discuss with your director what is appropriate. This is a tightrope to walk, though, because when a certain point is reached and too much information is being distributed, too many e-mails are sent, people start to ignore things, and even though the time and energy were spent to get all the important information into it, it just gets ignored. When possible, try to compile all information into a single e-mail and send it out at the end of the day. However, sometimes things just need to be sent out sooner, so use your best judgment.

Rehearsal Reminders

So, a beautiful rehearsal calendar has been created with everything color-coded and neatly laid out for easy comprehension. It has been distributed electronically and physically, and posted in multiple locations. Now everyone knows exactly the where and when of each rehearsal and there will be no confusion, right? We all wish. To help prevent the inevitable mistake, a daily rehearsal schedule should be sent out to the company (this should also be posted on the callboard). This notice should detail the day/date, location of rehearsal (include a street address if it is a new location), call times, and a general description of the rehearsal plan. This also makes a great platform to communicate last-minute schedule changes, make announcements, and generally keep everyone up to speed. Include the director, assistant stage managers, and any production team members who may be stopping by the rehearsal on these reminders as well. (You can include this information on the bottom of your rehearsal report for the production staff.)

Remember too that, at every rehearsal, it will be the stage manager's responsibility to keep track of the actors and make sure that everyone shows up when they are called. Starting about five minutes before each call time, check the sign-in sheet to insure everyone called is present (this includes your assistant stage manager(s) and the director!) and call anyone who is missing. Take tardiness seriously, as it can severely cut into rehearsal time and also wastes the time of all those who actually arrived when called.

Some theaters charge fines (or deduct them from paychecks) for things like tardiness or missed rehearsals. Look into the company's policy in one of your early meetings with either the staff or the director. Also note any tardiness or absences in your daily report. Fines may also cover other things like eating in costume or missing an entrance during a performance.

Prepping the Rehearsal Space

In order to properly prepare the rehearsal space, you should have a solid understanding of what will be happening in each rehearsal. Discuss with the director what their plan is for each rehearsal day (e.g., table reads, table work, first day on feet, first day blocking, etc.). Use this information to determine how to set up the rehearsal room each time. This is also a good time to start asking the director when they would like to start having rehearsal furniture/props, rehearsal costumes, etc. For more on types of rehearsals, see **Rehearsals** (p. 59).

Tape Out

Once the groundplan is finalized and before staging rehearsals begin, the set needs to be taped out. This simply means laying down tape on the rehearsal room floor outlining what the set will look like when it is built. This is to be done at full scale and with the exact dimensions noted on the groundplan. When working in a space that is not the one you will use for the show's run (i.e., a rehearsal space), it may also be helpful to tape out the dimensions of the performance stage. This helps the entire creative team envision the space they'll eventually be working in. In addition to the basic set, also mark out all non-sittable furniture and all large sittable furniture (e.g., desks, tables, couches, etc.).

> If the rehearsal space isn't large enough to tape out the entire set/theater, discuss with the director what they feel are the most important items to have taped out.

When doing a musical or show with heavy dance/choreography, it is advisable to also tape out dance numbers or quarters. Check with the choreographer to see if they have a preference. These divide the stage into easily visible equal sections and help the actors and choreographer with spacing.

To make dance numbers, make a mark at the centerline on the far downstage edge of the stage (see Figure 6.1a). This will serve as the "0" point. From there, make tick marks every two feet and tape out or write numbers at each of these marks (the marks two feet out from center should both be numbered "2," the next out will be "4," etc.). Make sure these numbers are large enough and facing in the correct direction for the actors to read from the stage. The choreographer may also want tick marks every foot, so ask for their preference. Depending on the complexity of the show, these numbers may also be required for performances. In that case, repeat this process on the stage after the floor treatment has been completed. These can also be painted on, depending on the floor treatment and the preference of the director.

Quarters are less visually obvious and are most common in dance (see Figure 6.1b). They divide the stage into quarters and eighths. After splitting the stage in half by marking center, continue to divide the stage into quarter and eighth segments. To do so mark a quarter halfway between center and the proscenium, then mark an onstage eighth between center and the quarter and then an offstage quarter between the quarter mark and the proscenium. Typically center and quarters are marked in one color of spike tape and are slightly larger marks, while the eighths are marked in a contrasting color and are slightly smaller.

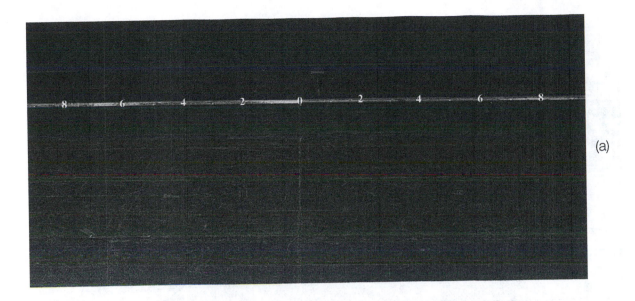

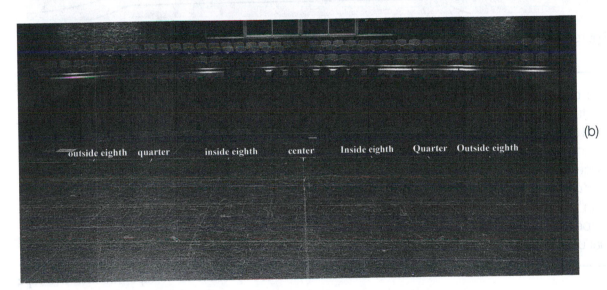

outside eighth   quarter   inside eighth   center   Inside eighth   Quarter   Outside eighth

Figure 6.1 a. An Example of Dance Numbers On a Stage, b. An Example of Quarters

When taping the stage or space, it is important that you use spike tape. Masking or other sorts of tape should never be used for this purpose. Spike tape comes off more easily than other kinds of tape and doesn't leave residue, while still remaining durable and long lasting. Additionally, it is available in a variety of colors; this comes in handy for color-coding different scenes or levels onstage. Check with the technical director for the theater's supply of spike tape, keeping in mind that more may need to be ordered. Always use what's needed to create an accurate tape out, but don't waste tape—it is expensive. It is a good idea to check and make sure the tape will indeed come off the floor without damaging it.

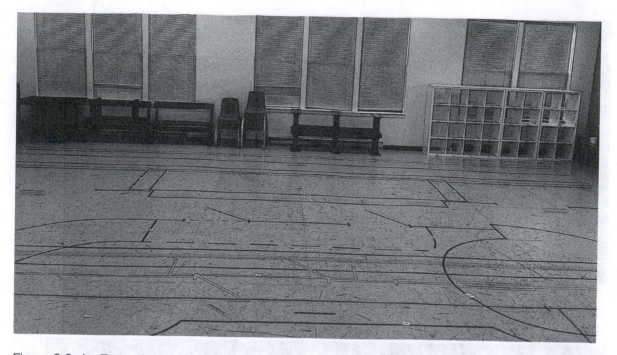

Figure 6.2 An Example of a Completed Tape Out

For designs that have moving wagons with multiple positions onstage, taping out each and every position can create a giant confusing web of spike tape. Instead, using a section of carpet or muslin that is cut to match the size and shape of the set piece can be very helpful. Be careful, though—depending on the floor surface and material used it can become slippery.

Tape out should be done prior to the first blocking/staging rehearsals (see Figure 6.2). Plan for it to take at least an hour. If it is a large or complex set, anticipate it taking longer.

Tools Required (See Figure 6.4)

a) Broom and dustpan
b) Spike tape (multiple colors)
c) Measuring tapes (ideally four)—two reel and two rigid (twenty-five feet or longer). It is possible to do tape out with two tape measures, but four is much easier
d) Architect's Scale ruler (used to take measurements off a scaled groundplan; if you don't own one or know how to use one, this is an important investment both in time and equipment—they can be purchased online or at many office supply stores)
e) Scale groundplan—quarter or half inch are the most typically used scales in the United States (see Figure 6.3).
   1) If you received an e-mail with a groundplan, this DOES NOT mean that it is to scale! See the technical director for a printed scale groundplan to work from. If you know how to use Vectorworks or AutoCAD, an updated file will also work. If you do not know how to use a CAD program, it is very beneficial to learn the basics.
   2) For faster taping, take time prior to tape out to plot key points on the groundplan. If you find the (x, y) coordinates of these points, you can easily plot them on the floor based off of the centerline (**y**) and the plaster line (**x**) and speed up the whole process (it is easiest to start with the "y" coordinate).

f) A framing square can be useful for your first few tape outs to help make sure your lines are straight.

g) A buddy (it is useful to have at least one other person to help!)

h) Music and snacks (this can be a lengthy process, so having some entertainment and food to make the time go faster can never hurt!)

Tape Out

Point	US (y axis)	SR/SL (x axis)	Direction	Notes
A	16'-3"	2'-0"	SR	Edge of Pit
B	24'-6"	8'-1"	SR	Top of SR Stairs
C	24'-4"	12'-2"	SR	
D	32'-2"	12'-2"	SR	
E	36'-6"	0'-0"	CTR	Peak of US Curve
F	32'-2"	12'-2"	SL	
G	21'-5"	9'-11"	SL	Top of SL Stairs - offstage
H	21'-5"	6'-11"	SL	Top of SL Stairs - onstage
I	16'-4"	9'-11"	SL	Connect to F
J	16'-4"	6'-11"	SL	Bottom of SL Stairs - onstage
K	16'-3"	2'-0"	SL	Edge of Pit
L	19'-10"	0'-0"	CTR	Peak of Pit
M				
N				
O				
P				
Q				
R				
S				
T				
U				
V				
W				
X				
Y				
Z				

Notes:
Stairs are all 1' Deep
DS Curve Radius = 4'-0"
Pit Radius = 2'-3"

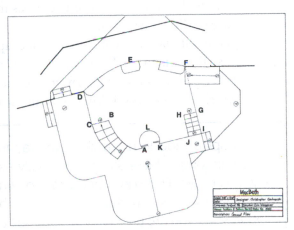

Figure 6.3 Example of Coordinates

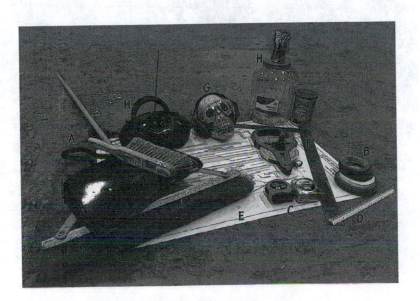

Figure 6.4 Tools Required for Tape Out

Taping Out

1) Thoroughly sweep the space prior to any taping! The tape will not stick well on a dusty floor. Even mopping may not be amiss.
2) Lay out reel measuring tapes marking the plaster line and the centerline.
   a) Tape down at either end and at the intersection point to keep in place. These will need to remain stationary throughout the tape out process.
3) Use the groundplan, your tape measure, and your previously plotted points to mark out key coordinates on the floor.
   a) Go up the centerline [the y axis] to the first coordinate and then measure out stage left or stage right to the other [x] coordinate. Measure from the plaster line (if you are using one) up to make sure the line stays even.
4) At each point place a small piece of spike tape.
5) Connect the dots to mark out the groundplan.
   a) Leave gaps to indicate doorways and include a strip of tape, imitating the door itself, to indicate which side the door is hinged on and which direction it opens.

> Cloth spike tape is more likely to stay in place for longer if it is stretched slightly as it is laid down. Pull tightly and press down firmly so that your marks will last through rehearsal! If you are using a non-cloth spike tape, make sure to use scissors to prevent the tape from curling up.

   b) Switch colors to indicate different levels or playing areas.
      i) If objects (platforms, for example) overlap, = you can use a dashed line for one and a solid line for the other.
      ii) As much as possible, make a color-coded plan prior to tape out, taking into account which colors and how much of each are on hand (see Figure 6.5).

Figure 6.5 A Basic Proscenium Tape Out Setup

Rehearsal Props/Furniture/Costumes

It is often the stage manager's job to pull rehearsal props and rehearsal furniture for the actors to use until the real props and furniture are available. These stand-ins should be about the same size and weight as the real thing so that the actors can become accustomed to working with them. Some theaters will require a sign-out sheet for items taken to rehearsal.

Having a prop that is close to the final prop is ideal; it is fine in many cases to use a stand-in if you don't have the desired prop on hand. For example, a block of wood of similar size and labeled for easy identification can make a perfect bar of soap or a book (see Figure 6.6). Remember that glass items have a strong tendency to break! For glassware and other fragile props, try to use plastic, acrylic, ceramic, and/ or otherwise sturdier materials until nearer to performance time.

It is important to have rehearsal furniture for blocking/staging rehearsals. This furniture, like the props, should be similar in shape and size to the final furniture (i.e., the rehearsal chair should have arms if the final chair will have arms). As much as possible, use the final furniture as it becomes available (and you have been given approval to use it), but it is very likely you will be using mostly stand-ins. Larger furniture can be represented by acting cubes or multiple chairs. Most theaters have a stock of furniture in storage that can be pulled for use in rehearsal.

It is important to remind your director that you are using rehearsal pieces. Sometimes they will make staging choices based on the rehearsal pieces that will not be relevant with the real prop or piece of furniture. This is a good reminder for the stage manager as well, as spike marks will need to be adjusted once the finalized pieces are in.

Figure 6.6 Example Rehearsal Props. A solo cup and a block of 2x4 each labeled for easy identification

Rehearsal costume pieces may be needed for the show as well: women may need skirts or corsets, men may need suit jackets or hats. The actors will need time to adjust to acting in this garb and it will have a large effect on blocking. Shoes also greatly affect movement and blocking for both sexes and rehearsal shoes may be employed early on to get the actors used to walking and dancing correctly. Talk to the costume designer or wardrobe supervisor (if one exists) and request rehearsal garb from them. This is something that is good to note early in the process. Some theaters will require a sign-out sheet for items taken to rehearsal. Unions have very specific rules when it comes to costume pieces, so make sure to check the regulations out ahead of time.

> If there will be a lot of physical activity for an actor, especially down on the floor, it is considerate to provide kneepads in rehearsal (kneepads may also be necessary in final costumes—keep your costume designer appraised, as this could affect the design and should be discussed in production meetings).

Prop Storage

All props (rehearsal and final) should be kept in a convenient, safe location; many rehearsal spaces and theaters have dedicated tables or cabinets that props can be stored in. It is very important to keep the props neat and organized. Labeling the table or shelves of a props cabinet either by piece or scene by scene (this can be done with masking tape or white gaff tape) will help actors put things back in the right spot and allow for quick and easy identification when something is missing.

Keep a props list (separated into scenes) with the props for reference. Update this list throughout the rehearsal process.

Many prop storages have locks on them because props have a habit of growing legs and wandering off. If this is the case, the storage needs to be locked every night, so make sure it is on the post-rehearsal checklist.

Stage Management Kit

A stage management kit is essentially a toolbox (most times literally) of basic supplies that might be necessary in rehearsal or in performance. Depending on the theater, a stage manager may use a personal kit or the theater may have one for use by the stage manager. If it is a personal kit, sometimes theaters will reimburse the stage manager for items taken from the kit. If it is the theater's kit, find out who is responsible for supplies and replenishment. It never hurts to ask!

Generic Kit Contents

- Pens/pencils/Sharpies/erasers/highlighters
- Refills of lead and erasers for mechanical pencils
- Notebook paper/notepads

- Hole reinforcers (donut stickers)
- Sticky notes
- Sticky arrows, tabs, flags
- Paperclips

- Rubber bands
- Spike tape
- Crescent wrench
- Screwdrivers (Phillips head and flat head)
- Flashlight
- Pocket knife
- Extension cord/power strip
- Hand sanitizer
- Tissues
- Lotion
- Tide spot cleaner
- Wet wipes
- Feminine products
- Bobbie pins
- Hair ties
- Cold pills
- Pain relievers (Ibuprofen and Tylenol)
- Band-Aids
- Ice packs
- Ace bandage
- Neosporin
- Disposable toothbrush/toothpaste
- Deodorant
- Dental floss
- Clear nail polish
- Hole punch
- Small stapler
- Scissors
- Tums/Pepto Bismol tablets
- CPR mask
- Non-drowsy allergy pills
- Glucose tablets
- Safety pins
- Mints/mouth spray (for actors)
- Cough drops
- Disposable razors
- Deck of cards
- Batteries
- Stress ball
- If your show involves children (or actors), coloring books and crayons/colored pencils (markers are not recommended)

Depending on the theater and local laws, the stage manager may not be legally allowed to dispense over-the-counter medications. They can, however, mention that the supplies exist and point folks in the right direction.

Light and Sound Systems

It is important for a stage manager to have a basic working knowledge of sound and light systems so they may be operated in their most basic form as needed for rehearsal and tech (see Figures 6.7 and 6.8). This also allows for better troubleshooting in the event that problems arise during a performance. Before tech rehearsals, meet with the technical director, lighting designer, and/or sound designer for a basic tutorial.

- Be able to operate and adjust a basic microphone
- Be able to operate the playback system—in many cases that is a computer playback system, but some theaters still use CDs or other methods
- Be able to turn on the lightboard and bring up lights
- Be able to replace a lamp

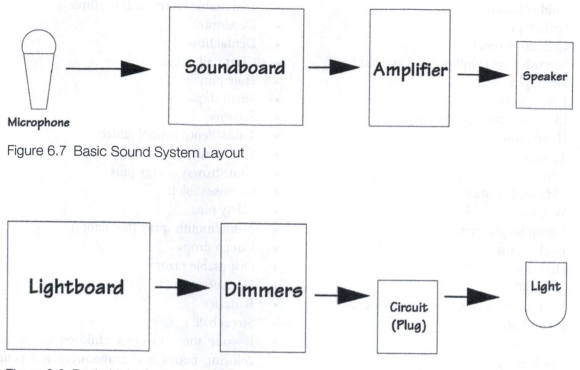

Figure 6.7 Basic Sound System Layout

Figure 6.8 Basic Light System Layout

Chapter Seven
Meetings

Concept Meetings

The initial concept meeting is the time when the director expresses the concept for the production. Sometimes the director will send a concept statement prior to the meeting for everyone to review and consider. Then, at the meeting, all of the designers can share their vision for the production and discuss ways of bringing their ideas to life. If the director's concept isn't introduced until the first meeting, then typically the design team will chat about their initial thoughts and feelings related to their research after hearing the director's concept. Sometimes this will happen during the meeting or in follow-up e-mails after the designers have had some time to digest it. Following those discussions another meeting will be scheduled for the designers to present their ideas to the director. Depending on the director, there may be many concept meetings, or perhaps only a few. Some directors like to have everyone meet once a week, while others like one-on-one meetings with each designer. Once the concept meetings have been concluded, it will be time to schedule regular production meetings. It is helpful to schedule a time for a weekly meeting even if it is not always going to be used; that way the time exists in everyone's schedule and, if it is needed, it is easy to have the meeting.

In many theaters not all of the design team may be local and will need to be phone or video conferenced in for meetings. Make sure to plan what method and technology will be used to do this and always test it before meeting time. Technology is a fickle beast; don't expect it to function properly.

Production Meetings

Production meetings serve as a regularly scheduled (typically weekly) check-in with all members of the production team. They will involve the sharing of sketches, progress reports, delays, challenges, problems, etc. The stage manager's attendance is mandatory. During the production meetings, it is the stage manager's responsibility to take detailed notes on everything discussed and to create a production meeting report. This is also the stage manager's chance to follow up on anything that has not been addressed from rehearsal reports.

Scheduling Meetings

Coordinating meetings typically falls to the stage manager. During the first meeting, it is usually best to arrange for a scheduled block of time each week to meet as needed. In the event a regular meeting time cannot be set, or if the director requires additional separate meetings, find a time that works with the schedules of all involved.

First, determine exactly who will need to attend the meetings. This is your production staff and usually includes the producer, artistic director, director, designers (scenic, costumes, lights, sound, projection), the props master/mistress, and the technical director. Assistant designers and assistant stage managers need not be present at meetings unless the designer expresses a desire for their attendance. For shows that involve music and/or dance/movement, these meetings will also include the music director and the choreographer. Depending on the company, they may also include the scenic charge, master carpenter, and/or the master electrician.

Some great online resources exist to help schedule meetings and find open times in people's schedules. Refer to the Online Resources section for more information.

Next, e-mail your production staff asking for their weekly schedules. Compile their responses and find an open hour. Assign the determined hour as your weekly production meeting time. Announce this time to your production staff as soon as possible.

Sometimes you will have to leave one or more people out due to conflicts. Determine this on a case-by-case basis. In these cases, find out if it is possible to include missing team members via conference call or video. If they are unable to participate at all, ask for any items that need to be discussed regarding their department. During the meeting, carefully record any information pertinent to them, as well as any questions that need their immediate attention. (This is one of the reasons why taking good notes is so important.)

When reaching out to the production team about their schedules, also request their preferred contact information. If you already have their contact information, confirm this. You will want to have a contact sheet put together before your first concept/production meeting so it can be distributed. Additionally, make a point to input all contact information into your phone or other readily available location. As the communication center of the production, you will frequently be called upon to contact the other members of the team, so having this information easily accessible is a must.

For those working in an academic setting, preferred e-mails and contact information may be non-university/college e-mails, as academic systems have a habit of being unreliable. It is not a bad idea as a stage manager to set up a "work" or "professional" (something other than ilovepandas@example.com) Gmail, Yahoo, or other mail account to insure communication stays flowing. Always remember to check and keep up with your inbox.

Prior to Meetings

Send out an e-mail reminder twenty-four hours prior to the meeting including the time, date, and location of the meeting. Many calendar programs allow for invites to be sent to all parties, which will add the event to their calendars and push reminders to those who have push notifications on.

Create an agenda for each meeting. These should have a section for each department (i.e., scenic, costumes, props, etc.) and include discussion points and questions. If you don't have anything specific for a department, you should still give them a chance to voice questions and/or concerns. If an item pertains to only one department, you may decide to arrange a meeting between the director and that department in order to keep production meetings productive for all involved. Although many times, it is helpful for all of the departments to share in the discussions. Have copies of the agenda on hand for all involved parties, including yourself.

When compiling the agenda, also look back at previous rehearsal and production meeting reports for any unanswered questions that may have come up or items or discussion points that were tabled from previous meetings.

Time estimates are beneficial to help judge if a meeting is on track. This is optional, but a good skill to work on. After a while, it will become second nature to you, but it is a skill that takes time and practice. By estimating prior to meetings, you can keep meetings on track and also learn by trial and error how long meetings and certain discussions will last. Including a time estimate for each department will also allow for a total meeting time to be calculated. These time estimates should be for your use only—don't include them on the distributed copy of the agenda (see Appendix G).

Running a Meeting

Your use of this section should be based upon your previous conversation with the director (if they are running the meeting or you are).

If possible, arrive at least ten minutes early to allow time to set up and get everyone assembled. If any team members are missing or late, it will be the stage manager's responsibility to call them and find out where they are. Begin the meeting on time and start by asking the director if they have any general comments or questions to bring to the table. Go department by department and give each designer time to talk and ask questions regarding their aspect of the show. Follow the agenda; it is a great tool to keep meetings on track and on time. If people begin to go off topic, it is your job to gently bring the conversation back to where it needs to be. At the end of each department's discussion, make sure that all agenda items have been answered (or at least addressed and, if necessary, tabled for later discussion) and ask if there is anything else for that department. If everything has been discussed, move promptly on to the next department.

If a topic requires extensive discussion and only involves one or two departments, consider tabling the conversation and scheduling a separate meeting. It is courteous to the other members of the production

It is a nice gesture to rotate the order meeting to meeting, so the same department isn't always waiting their turn and potentially being short-changed each meeting by coming at the end when everyone is ready to go or time is cut short. When possible utilize a round table—it promotes equality and collaboration.

team and will help keep focus within meetings. These meetings should always include the stage manager, the director, and all relevant departments. However, use discretion when deciding to schedule a separate meeting. Often a topic that only seems relevant to one department may in fact affect the whole production team.

At the end of the meeting, ask once more if there are any other items of business that need to be addressed (particularly in areas that may not have representatives, i.e., front of house). End the meeting with a reminder of the time, date, and location of the next meeting. As soon as possible after the meeting, send out production meeting notes. These should go out no later than the following morning. The sooner, the better!

"Only if you want to attend," is a phrase often used. Always attend if you are able and come prepared to take notes. Many people claim to take good notes and that they will distribute them, but it is better if they come from a centralized person, namely, the stage manager.

Occasionally, it will be beneficial and/or necessary to hold a department-specific meeting (e.g., props meeting, costume check-in). Typically stage management will coordinate these. Depending on the nature of the meeting, the stage manager's presence may or may not be required. Check with everyone involved, especially the director, to see if they would like the stage manager there and schedule the meeting accordingly. It is advisable to attend all meetings if possible.

Meeting Notes and Reports

After the meeting, use the aforementioned detailed notes you have taken and generate a report. Create a meeting report template during prep week for this purpose and use consistent formatting with each distributed report for easy reading.

Information to Include in Every Report

Every report should contain basic identifiers including show title, name of stage manager, time and date of meeting, time and date of next meeting, people present, and a distribution list. The body of the report should contain detailed notes on anything and everything discussed. It is extremely important to take thorough notes at every meeting. The notes need to be comprehensible, clear, and formatted for easy reading. They will be referenced throughout the production process as a reminder of what and how decisions were made, which decisions were tabled, as well as to inform anyone not present at the meeting of what was discussed. Separate notes by department (e.g., scenic notes under a scenic section, props under props, etc.). Include notes that affect multiple departments in each of those sections (this should also be a practice used when writing rehearsal reports), e.g., a note about a cane or hat may fall under costumes and props.

Be precise and concise in the distributed report. Take more elaborate notes for yourself during the meeting and then distill them down for the distributed report. Keep an original copy of your detailed notes for reference. If a department or field does not have a note or any information it is important to place text in that field to the effect of "There are no notes at this time" to insure that the field was not accidently left blank. It is to your advantage to take notes on all items discussed, even ideas that are decided against. Should a problem arise with the decision, there is a record of the other ideas that were thrown around so you don't have to re-brainstorm. When in doubt, write it down! (See Appendix H.)

General note about paperwork: whenever you distribute any paperwork electronically, it is good practice to send it in PDF form. This helps prevent any format changes or accidental editing on the part of the recipient. Only send editable versions of things when you intend them to be edited. Additionally, copy and paste paperwork contents into the body of your e-mail as well as attaching a PDF version. Your co-workers are more likely to read it if they don't have to open an attachment and there is less possibility of faulty documents impeding the process. Be sure to always double-check formatting and accuracy of information before distributing.

Chapter Eight
Rehearsals

Types of Rehearsals

Typically, the very first rehearsal for a play will consist of a table read, in which the whole cast sits around a table and reads through the entire script, each reading his or her role. The stage manager may be asked to read the stage directions aloud or provide sound effects. The director may elect to do this instead—determine this before the rehearsal begins. Be sure to time all read-throughs of the script. This will give a frame of reference for approximately how long the play will be once it is in performance. Invite designers to this rehearsal. This is a great time for them to meet the cast, get to hear the script out loud, and give a brief presentation on their preliminary design ideas.

Another type of rehearsal that may take place in the first week or two is called table work. Similar to a table read, these rehearsals are also seated. The goal is typically to work slowly through the script, stopping to talk about character, pacing, story background, etc. For any table work rehearsals (including the table read), it is courteous to come prepared with plenty of pencils, pens, highlighters, and pencil sharpeners.

If you are working on a musical your first rehearsal may be a sing-through. If not on the first day, this will likely happen sometime during the first week. This is much like a read-through but with the music and typically run by the music director. For this rehearsal, a piano or keyboard and the rehearsal accompanist will be necessary, so prepare accordingly (e.g., have the piano tuned). If they are available, music stands can be very helpful so that the actors can group around the piano or keyboard and still have a place for their scripts.

The other type of rehearsal inherent to musicals will be, of course, music rehearsals. Coordinate with the director and the music director about when these rehearsals will take place. On those days, a piano or keyboard will need to be provided. Chairs gathered around the piano should be provided for the actors as well. Mostly, music rehearsals are pretty hands-off for the stage manager. This is the time for the music director to work on notes, style, and technique with the actors. In these rehearsals, the stage manager is there to monitor breaks, keep track of time, and lend a hand when help is required. This is a good time to get familiar with the music and expectations of the music director to help you with calling and maintaining the show later in the process. Sometimes, music rehearsals will take place simultaneously with staging rehearsal in order to increase the efficiency of rehearsal time. In these cases, a separate room will need to be reserved. Ideally, there should be a member of stage management present in each rehearsal room. However, music rehearsals tend to be very self-sufficient. If you are working on a show solo and have simultaneous music and staging rehearsals, always attend the staging rehearsal.

Once table work has been completed, the actors will get on their feet. Sometimes, they will jump directly into blocking, typically starting at the top (beginning) of the show. Other times, there may be a day of movement in which the director and choreographer (if there is one) will run through some exercises to see how the actors move and interact together. This is typical for shows with dance or choreography, or in highly stylized pieces. For these rehearsals, a clear rehearsal room is best. For blocking rehearsals, be sure to come in with all previously agreed upon rehearsal furniture, props, and costumes (if applicable) and have the floor taped out in preparation.

Logistics for Musical Rehearsals

A crucial aspect of rehearsals for musicals is staging and choreographing musical numbers. Depending on the production, you may be working with a rehearsal pianist or with pre-recorded rehearsal tracks.

If you are working with a rehearsal pianist, there are a few things you need to add to your to do list. First, be sure to include the pianist in your schedule distribution list. Note specifically which rehearsals they will be required to attend and what time (if they will not be utilized for the entire rehearsal). As much as possible, give them a heads-up as to what will be worked on at each rehearsal as well as the type of rehearsal it will be (they will need to prepare differently for a first-time choreography rehearsal than for a run-through of a full act). Additionally, you will need to coordinate with your rehearsal space and your producer to provide a piano or keyboard at all musical rehearsals. If it is a piano, check that it is reasonably in tune. If it is a keyboard, be sure that power, cords, and any necessary amplification are accessible in the rehearsal room.

If a rehearsal pianist is unavailable or if there is not the budget for it, you will need to have rehearsal tracks. The best way to do this is to coordinate with the music director to record all musical numbers. Ideally, this will all be done in one session. However, if the recording needs to be in multiple sessions, prioritize according to the rehearsal schedule. If the official recording matches the score, you can work from the cast album. Either a recording or a pianist MUST be available at the time the number is rehearsed. When using rehearsal tracks be sure to have speakers or access to the sound system so that tracks will be loud enough to be heard by all while singing in full voice.

The combined script and vocal score used for most musicals is called a libretto, the plural of which is libretti.

Running a Rehearsal

Daily Rehearsal Prep

Immediately prior to every rehearsal, there is a certain amount of preparation that stage management must complete. The specifics of this preparation are, of course, dependent on the company, the director, the space, and the type of rehearsal taking place, but the basics remain the same. Arrive at every rehearsal prepped with the promptbook, stage management kit, stopwatch, something to take notes on (electronic or paper), your phone, and a positive attitude.

Unlock and Turn On

The stage manager is almost always the first person in the space. Arrive at least forty-five minutes prior to rehearsal to allow time for preparation. First, unlock doors (outside, rehearsal room, bathrooms, green room, dressing rooms, etc.), and turn on lights and sound systems (if applicable). Update the callboard. This is also a good time to check supplies in the bathrooms and first aid kits. While you won't necessarily be accountable for replacing these items, you should contact the technical director or space coordinator if supplies are running low.

If you have assistant stage managers, they should arrive at this time as well. Take a couple of minutes to talk through the schedule for the rehearsal and assign responsibilities for the day (who is taking blocking notes, who is monitoring actor arrivals, who is tracking props, etc.).

Clean the Rehearsal Space

For safety and out of consideration for the actors, do a thorough sweep of the space before each rehearsal. A good sweeping is especially necessary if rehearsal takes place on the stage where scenery is in the process of being built (common for academic productions), as wood splinters, stray screws, and other potential safety hazards can remain after a day of shop work. If actors will be barefoot or on the floor, mop the space as well. Pick up any trash and generally tidy up. This is essentially the production's office, so make the space presentable. A clean, welcoming room will better foster productivity, creativity, and positive attitudes.

Prep Your Workstation

Set up a table facing the playing area, ideally close to the door. This will be to seat stage management and the director, as well as any visiting designers, choreographers, etc. who may be sitting in on rehearsal. Run a power strip to the table. The stage manager is up and down constantly throughout rehearsal, so settle in a place where you can easily get in and out without being disruptive. The director should also be set up in such a place. Include a cup with extra pencils, pens, and highlighters for the actors to borrow. It is also a good idea to keep a box of tissues on the table.

Review the rehearsal schedule for the day and keep a copy next to your promptbook for easy reference. Open your promptbook to the first section being worked on, prep a blank sheet of paper or document for notes, and prep your station with a pen, pencil(s), and an eraser. Have a blank rehearsal report ready to fill in as rehearsal goes along. Keep your stage manager's kit nearby and pull out commonly used items for quick access (for rehearsals, these would be spike tape, gaff tape, sticky notes/tabs, Scotch tape, and spare paper).

Make sure that your computer is set at an angle to you when it is open during rehearsal. It seems silly, but if you place it directly in front of you it acts as a virtual barrier between the cast and you, and that is not something you want to create. You'll also want to be able to see past it to take blocking.

First Rehearsal Paperwork

If it is the first rehearsal, there is some extra paperwork that you should bring for distribution:

- Contact sheet (one copy)—pass around for people to double-check info, then update before the next rehearsal for distribution. If it is already updated and accurate, bring enough copies to distribute to the full cast (including the director and assistant stage managers).
- Sign-in sheet (see Appendix I)
- Emergency contact forms (these are typically theater specific)—have the actors fill these out sometime during the rehearsals (either on a break or if they have downtime) and return to you before the end of the day. These should include dietary restrictions and allergy information as well as any pertinent medical information.
  - Take this into account when planning for any edible props or company meals.
- Copies of the company handbook (if one exists)
- Relevant rehearsal/company information (e.g., parking maps, dramaturgical research packets, etc.)—bring enough copies to distribute to the full cast.
- Rehearsal schedule—enough copies for everyone present, including yourself
- Scripts (if they haven't already been distributed/picked up)
  - If they are being returned at the end of the show, number them and have a sign-out sheet to keep track of them.
  - Include a damage waiver if applicable.
  - Keep a copy of the sign-out sheet in your promptbook for easy reference and in case of lost/destroyed scripts.

At all times, keep at least one extra copy of the script in your stage management kit. If the script goes through any revisions, keep this copy updated as well. This will serve as a backup in case anyone forgets or loses their script, if any new members join the cast, for any stand-in actors (such as an assistant stage manager) during a rehearsal where the primary actor is absent, or for a designer/choreographer/producer to look at while sitting in on a rehearsal.

Prep the Rehearsal Space

Discuss with the director ahead of time what will be happening during this rehearsal so proper setup can be planned. Set up chairs and tables if table work or a read-through is planned. If blocking is planned, make sure the space is properly taped out and all the rehearsal furniture is easily accessible. Set up chairs outside the playing area for the actors to set their belongings on and to sit when they aren't onstage.

Check Attendance

Ten minutes before rehearsal is scheduled to begin, check the sign-in sheet to see which actors have arrived. Start calling those who haven't yet checked in to confirm they are on their way. Establish early on that being on time for rehearsal is of the utmost importance, as any delay can take away from what is already a precious amount of rehearsal time. Encourage all of the company members to maintain open communication with you and to always contact you if they know they will be late to rehearsal. It still isn't good for them to be late, but if you know ahead of time, you and the director can adjust the rehearsal plan accordingly.

Start Rehearsal

When it is time for rehearsal to begin, close the door to the space (if possible), posting a sign on the outside stating "Quiet please, rehearsal in progress." Call the company to attention, announce the start of rehearsal, and give a quick reminder about the plan for the day. If the director wants to jump right in, have the actors set for the scene being worked on. If they want to speak with the company first, pass the attention to the director and let them take over the rehearsal.

> A dual purpose can be served by using cell phones as a way of signing in. Labeling the pockets on a clear multi-pocket shoe rack with each cast member's name and asking them to put their cell phone in the pocket to indicate that they are present, gives you a quick visual way to see who is present, as well as minimizing digital distractions in the rehearsal room. Be sure that the shoe rack is in a secure location and easily visible to protect phones from theft or loss.

During Rehearsal

By this point, you and the director should have discussed how rehearsals will be run and what your role will be. The stage manager's primary job is to support the director by running an efficient, smooth, and productive rehearsal to accomplish the work expected for the day. This relationship will develop over time as you each grow accustomed to your working relationship. Whatever happens, never get into an argument or a major disagreement in front of the rest of the company. Let the director take the lead and keep rehearsal moving forward. Pull them aside after rehearsal (or, if absolutely necessary, during a break) to work out any issues privately.

Take Notes

So much happens during rehearsal and the only way to keep track of it all is to write it down. Never assume you will be able to remember something. There is no reason to allow something to be overlooked or forgotten about because you relied on your memory rather than jotting down a quick note.

Rehearsal Report Notes

One of the stage manager's responsibilities during rehearsal is to create a rehearsal report. This will lay out anything important that occurs in rehearsal, as well as any notes that need to be passed on to the various departments. This includes any added props, any repairs that need to be addressed, any blocking notes that could affect costumes, set, etc., script changes (including cuts/additions) that will affect costumes or lighting, etc. A section should be provided that includes the original rehearsal plan and a summary of what was actually worked, as well as start, end, and break times. Any injuries, late arrivals, unexcused absences, or unusual circumstances should also be noted in these reports.

Prep a new report at the start of each rehearsal and add notes as they come up. It will be easier than trying to remember everything at the end and that way nothing will be left out accidentally.

Approach the director at the end of each rehearsal to review the report together and to see if they have any additional information that they would like add before sending it out. These are distributed to all members of the production team, but not the cast. Be sure to send out all rehearsal reports the same day or before the start of the work day the following day (see Appendix J).

Use your best judgment when choosing what should be included in the rehearsal report. Many times actors will come up to you with questions about what they will be wearing or what their prop will be; unless this is a question from the director as well, do not include it in the rehearsal report. You can ask the director the question and if they don't know and/or want to know then it can be added to the report.

Personal Notes

Take note of any action items for yourself. This may be a reminder to send out the new fitting schedule, to look up the correct pronunciation of a foreign word in the script, or to buy more sticky notes.

Script Notes

There are two types of scriptural notes: blocking notes and script notes. Blocking is a record of the movements the actors make, and script notes track any changes in the script.

Recording Blocking

The key to blocking is to find a system in which one can write as little and as quickly as possible while still being able to interpret what is written. Be precise. The first step is to create a shorthand key (see Figure 8.1). Include character abbreviations (which may be circled). All stage directions should be in all caps. Create shorthand for all furniture pieces, as well as any entrance/exit locations.

Prior to the start of blocking rehearsals, print out a copy of the groundplan and split the stage into sections: USL, USC, USR, SL, CS, SR, DSL, DSC, and DSR (depending on your set, you can choose to split the groundplan into greater or fewer sections). Use this as a reference while you take blocking notes in order to be as precise as possible.

All notes taken in the script should be written in pencil. Come to every rehearsal with multiple pencils, some large erasers (the white Pentel hi-polymer or Staedtler Plastic erasers work very well), extra paper, and some patience. The blocking **will** change and there will be a lot of erasing and updating as progress is made. Never write blocking in pen.

Margin Notation Method

One method of recording blocking is to write it directly in the margins of the script (see Figure 8.2). Next to the line where the actor moved, write down in shorthand their path and where they end up. This method tends to take up a large amount of space in the margins, which can make it difficult to also

Macbeth Blocking Key:

Cast:

MB	– Macbeth
LB	– Lady Macbeth
BQ	– Banquo
FL	– Fleance
ML	– Malcolm
DB	– Donalbain
MD	– Macduff
LD	– Lady Macduff
LN	– Lennox
RS	– Ross
MN	– Menteith
AG	– Angus
CN	– Caithness
SI	– Siward
SG	– Sargent
PR	– Porter
W1	– Witch 1
W2	– Witch 2
W3	– Witch 3
DR	– Doctor
JS	– Justin
DV	– Dave
TM	– Tom
AN	– Andy
JN	– Jenn

Entrances:

SL-A	– Stage Left Around the masking wall
SL-D	– Stage Left through the Doorway
SR-A	– Stage Right Around the masking wall
SR-D	– Stage Right through the Doorway
CAL	– Enter from the Cauldron Center
SL-H	– Stage Left House/apron
SR-H	– Stage Right House/apron
DH	– Down House through the audience aisle
UCL	– Up Center Left – between standing stones
UCR	– Up Center Right – between standing stones

Misc.:

@	– At
&	– And
↓	– Sit
↑	– Stand
→	– Then/next
↳	– Concurrent action
X	– Cross
EXT	– Exit
ENT	– Entrance
L	– Lights up
B/O	– Blackout

Figure 8.1 Blocking Shorthand

ACT II

SCENE I. Court of Macbeth's castle.

[margin: IN B/O BQ EN SL-D ↓ L OF C @ WALL]

Enter BANQUO, and FLEANCE bearing a torch before him SR-A

BANQUO
How goes the night, boy?

[margin: PLAYING INNOCENT]

FLEANCE
The moon is down; I have not heard the clock.

BANQUO   *[margin: BQ ↑]*
And she goes down at twelve.

FLEANCE
I take't, 'tis later, sir.

[margin: BQ HAND FL SWORD]

BANQUO
Hold, take my sword. There's husbandry in heaven;

[margin: BQ HAND FL DAGGER]

Their candles are all out. Take thee that too.
A heavy summons lies like lead upon me,
And yet I would not sleep: merciful powers,

[margin: BQ TURN TO EXT SL-D FL START TO FOLLOW]

Restrain in me the cursed thoughts that nature
Gives way to in repose!

[margin: BQ TURN]

Enter MACBETH, and a Servant with a torch SR-D *[margin: PR]*

Give me my sword. FL HANDS
Who's there?

MACBETH
A friend.

[margin: BQ SWORD BACK TO FL]

BANQUO
What, sir, not yet at rest? The king's a-bed:
He hath been in unusual pleasure, and
Sent forth great largess to your offices.
This diamond he greets your wife withal,

[margin: BQ X TO MS FL COUNTER]

By the name of most kind hostess; and shut up
In measureless content.

MACBETH
Being unprepared,
Our will became the servant to defect;
Which else should free have wrought.

BANQUO
All's well.
I dreamt last night of the three weird sisters:
To you they have show'd some truth.

MACBETH
I think not of them:
Yet, when we can entreat an hour to serve,
We would spend it in some words upon that business,
If you would grant the time.

BANQUO
At your kind'st leisure.

MACBETH

[margin: MB CLAP BQ ON SHOULDER]

If you shall cleave to my consent, when 'tis,
It shall make honour for you.

BANQUO
So I lose none
In seeking to augment it, but still keep
My bosom franchised and allegiance clear,
I shall be counsell'd.

MACBETH
Good repose the while!

BANQUO

[margin: BQ & MB HUG]

Thanks, sir: the like to you!

[margin: BQ & FL EXT SL-D]

Figure 8.2 Margin Notation Method

use that same script as the calling script. However, if blocking or the cues are light or if you don't mind having two separate scripts in the promptbook, this is a very viable and commonly used option. It is also a good method to use when first becoming acclimated to taking blocking, as it involves the fewest steps.

Groundplan and Numbering Method

Another method of recording blocking is to use a groundplan and numbered movements tracking sheet (see Figure 8.3). With this method, print a small groundplan on the back of each script page and include

> Taking blocking notes is something that will improve with time and practice. Use these guidelines as a starting place and then find a method that works best for you. What is important is that it is legible and can be deciphered by anyone who picks up the promptbook.

space to write down your blocking. Write a number next to the line in the script where the actor moved and, on the opposite page under the groundplan, write the number and their movement in your blocking shorthand. Use the groundplan to plot a particularly complicated set of movements or a strange path followed. The groundplan is also very useful for large group scenes in order to keep track of lots of characters at once.

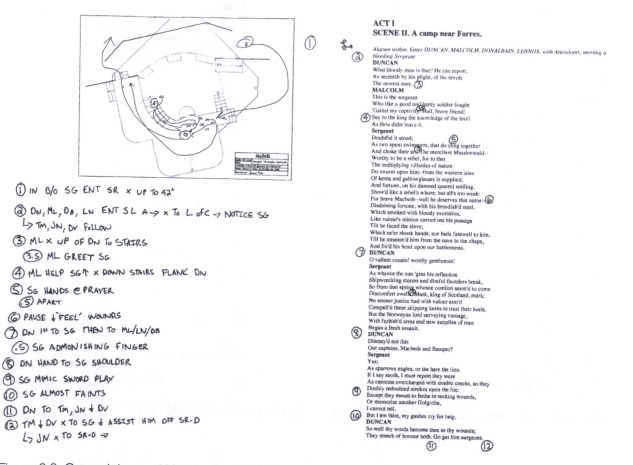

Figure 8.3 Groundplan and Numbering Method

Pictures and Video Recording Blocking

When working on a musical or other large production, it can be difficult to keep track of blocking/choreography/fights (there is only one of you and so many of them!!!). A helpful trick is to take a video of the rehearsal. Record large group numbers, complicated choreography, and fight rehearsals. These can be used to help accurately check blocking, as well as a reminder for directors/choreographers. The stage manager can also distribute videos to the cast as a guide. These should be updated whenever the blocking changes, just as with your normal blocking notes. Sometimes it is useful to take pictures of large group scenes where it will take too much time to write down everyone's names—go back and look at these after rehearsal to update your script.

Before recording any rehearsals, check with your director and/or producer. If you are working with union actors or in a union house (Actors' Equity Association or otherwise), it is strictly against code to video or audio record ANY rehearsals. You also need to be cautious about distribution of the videos, to avoid any issues with copyright infringement. Any recorded material should be distributed for use by only the actors and the production team.

> Learning the basics of video software will allow you to size down the videos so they do not take up as much space. Another good way to save space and ease sharing is to create a private YouTube group and post all videos there. Make sure you have permission from your director and choreographer before posting.

Tracking Script Changes

Generally, for artistic integrity and copyright purposes, no changes should be made to the script. However, if you are working on a new piece or directly with a playwright, it is possible that script changes will be made during the rehearsal process. In these cases, it may fall to the stage manager to keep track of any and all of these changes. Note them in the script, make announcements of all permanent changes to everyone (including the production team, as script changes can affect them as well!), and keep a running document noting the change and the date the change was made. Be sure to keep this document updated and available for perusal in case anyone has questions or missed a change.

> If you are working on a very new work, there may be large changes. It can be helpful to copy each set of changes on a different color of paper—that way you can easily make sure everyone is always using the same version. Additionally, always include the date and a version number in the header or footer of the changed pages. As small changes occur, you should date those on the page as well.

Technical Notes

Rehearsals are also the time when the director discovers the reality of the production. This is when prop lists are revised, light and sound cues are discovered, and set requirements are updated. Keep note of any and all things the director says in regards to anything technical. This particular task can be tough for first-time stage managers and is a skill that definitely develops over time and with experience. It requires strong focus, multitasking skills, and detailed note taking. Don't get too frustrated if you aren't able

> Throughout the rehearsal process, keep a post-it note on the first blocking page of each scene. As work through the scenes in rehearsal progresses, jot down all set pieces and props needed for the scene and any props/set pieces that are in the previous scene that need to be struck. Once runs or scene change blocking begins this can easily be referenced to make sure everything is accounted for. This will also make compiling run-sheets much easier!
>
> Keep track of where props come on and go off as you work through rehearsals. This will make your preset list and prop tracking easier throughout the run of the show.

to get everything down. Write what you can and take note of the items you need to follow up on. Go over these notes with the director at the end of the night because sometimes they say things in the spur of the moment that they later decide they don't want or they were joking about.

Keep Rehearsal on Time and Monitor Breaks

Much like production meetings, it will fall to the stage manager to keep track of the time and keep the rehearsal as close to schedule as possible. Give gentle reminders to the director when you are nearing a break or the scheduled time to move on to a new scene or task. Agree on the best way to do this prior to the start of rehearsals (sometimes it is verbal, sometimes with hand signals, or a note passed on the tech table). Avoid giving these reminders in the middle of a scene or during a speech from the director. For many directors, this will take them out of the moment or derail their train of thought, which is frustrating. This is another skill that you will develop over time and will vary (sometimes dramatically) from director to director.

The director will also look to you to keep the rehearsal focused. Help keep side conversations and noise to a minimum and rein in the focus onstage if the action derails or if the director digresses too much during a speech. Rehearsals should be fun, but also productive. Jokes and hilarious line flubs can and will happen. It is fine (and important!) to allow the company to enjoy these moments. However, don't be afraid to step in with a gentle "Focus, please!" after they've had a moment of fun and keep the rehearsal moving forward.

Breaks

It is important to give the actors breaks during rehearsals. Union rules state that breaks must be provided according to the following breakdown: a five-minute break for every fifty-five minutes of rehearsal or a ten-minute break for every eighty minutes. Many companies follow these guidelines, whether they are union or not, but discuss this with the director and the producer (if applicable) prior to the start of rehearsals. Keep an eye on the time so that breaks occur as required and set a timer so rehearsal can start again as soon as possible.

> Sometimes a director's preference for break times will vary depending on what they are working. In dance rehearsals it is often best to use the five after fifty-five rule to keep the dancers fresh, but if they are doing "meaty" character work or blocking a large scene it may make more sense to work for eighty minutes and then take a longer break.

Monitor Staggered Actor Calls

Just as at the start of rehearsal, check in ten minutes before any actor calls to make sure they have arrived or are on their way. Also, keep open communication with the director about releasing actors early who will not be needed for the full rehearsal. Never release an actor without the permission of the director. Similarly, no actor should ever leave the rehearsal without being released by the stage manager. Make this point clear at the first rehearsal.

Set Changes

Since the rehearsals are unlikely to have a tech crew of any kind, it will fall to stage management to make any scene changes. These often occur during breaks or need to happen quickly to keep the rehearsal moving forward. Execute these as quickly and as accurately as possible, including props and costumes as necessary. Make sure to dress appropriately for rehearsal to be able to quickly and safely accomplish the changes.

If rehearsing in the same space as the scenery is being built, the director will likely want to rehearse with set pieces as soon as possible. Always check with the technical director before using any set pieces. Pieces may look complete, but may be unsafe for the actors or too fragile to be worked with.

Spiking

Once furniture is set in place on the stage, it is stage management's duty to spike each piece with spike tape. This will allow for easy and accurate placement of furniture as it moves from scene to scene and for when it needs to be placed for rehearsal. Spike furniture at the end of rehearsal before striking it for the evening or within the rehearsal once the director is happy with placement. Use different colors of tape for each separate scene or locale (as much as possible) and keep a record of which color is for which scene.

To spike, rip or cut two small pieces (approx. 1 inch each) of spike tape and stick them together to make a right angle. Use these to frame the upstage corners of the furniture/set piece (chair legs, platform corners, etc.). For abnormal-shaped pieces, mark all four sides. For most chairs and tables, marking the two upstage legs will be enough. For smaller chairs and tables, especially those where the angle of the furniture piece doesn't matter, sometimes it is better to mark an "X" directly at the center of its placement, rather than marking legs.

If furniture placement changes, be sure to move the spikes or make new spike marks. Be sure to remove all old spike marks in order to avoid confusion! Sometimes it is helpful to write directly on the spike tape what each spike is for. Use a Sharpie or another thick pen so that you can read it.

In the UK spike tape is typically a vinyl tape similar to electrical tape; it is very important to use scissors to cut this type of tape to prevent the ends from curling up.

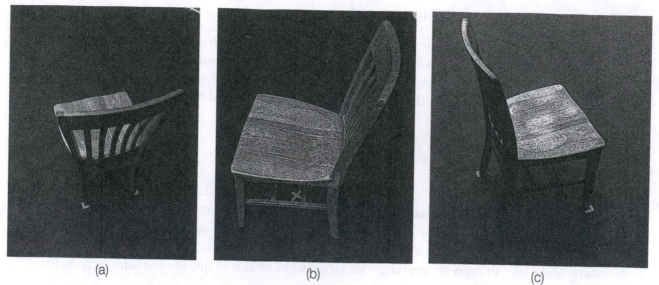

(a)

(b)

(c)

(d)

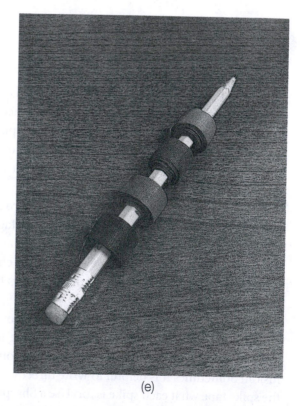

(e)

Figure 8.4 a. Normal Upstage Spike Mark, b. Centered Spike Mark, c. Alternate Corner Spike Mark, d. Labeled Spike, e. Spike Stick

As mentioned, it is a good idea to use a different color of spike tape for each different scene. Pick these colors carefully, according to their purpose. For rehearsals, bright, bold colors are best (yellow, pink, orange, light blue) or, if the rehearsal space has light-colored floors, dark colors for contrast. For most shows, it is preferable not to see the spike marks onstage, so you should stick to darker colors and ones that can blend into the floor color (but not so much that you can't find the mark!), especially in raked houses where the floor can be more easily seen by the audience. For scene changes that occur in darkness, it is better to use brighter colors that will be easier to find (blues and light greens are nice for this). You may even use glow tape to mark these, if finding the spike mark in the dark is too difficult.

> Some stage managers use a "spike stick," which is a stick (dowel, pencil, chopstick, etc.) that can have multiple colors of spike tape and be carried more easily than numerous rolls of spike tape. To make a spike stick you create a mini roll of tape by wrapping it around the pencil—some people have a different stick for each variety of tape (neons, naturals, lights, darks, etc.). See Figure 8.4 for an example.

> It is surprisingly common to work with actors/crew members who are colorblind. Determine this early on so that you can choose spike colors accordingly.

After Rehearsal

Actor Dismissal

Thank everyone for their work and cooperation for the day. Give a quick reminder about the time/location of the next rehearsal, as well as what will be rehearsed (if this hasn't changed due to the current rehearsal) and any other important notices/reminders.

Director Check-in

Have a five to ten minute check-in with the director once the actors have left. Go through your personal notes to clarify any questions or give them any reminders. Go through the rehearsal report together and see if they have anything to add. Confirm the next rehearsal schedule and if they have any specific tasks/requests that need to be fulfilled before that time. Thank them for a good rehearsal and wish them goodnight.

Complete and Distribute the Rehearsal Report

Add any final notes from the director, making sure all notes are clear and concise. Double-check that all of your information, including headings, is accurate and up to date. Distribute the report as soon as possible. As with all distributed documents, always send it in PDF form so as to avoid any formatting issues or accidental changes to the document.

Distribute Rehearsal Reminder

E-mail the cast with a reminder of the time, location, and summary of the planned work for the next rehearsal, as well as any important notices/reminders given at rehearsal and as requested by the director.

Clean Up the Space

Put away all props and rehearsal furniture. Clean up your table. Leave the space the way you found it, especially if it is a borrowed or rented space. If the rehearsal space will be used exclusively by your company during the run of your production, speak with the technical director or space coordinator about how much must be struck (put away) each night. In some cases, the table and some furniture can remain in the space, making for a simpler rehearsal setup each night.

Close Down

Shut off lights and sound systems, take down rehearsal signs, and lock the doors.

First Rehearsal Off-Book

When creating the rehearsal schedule, or sometime in the early days of the rehearsal process, establish with the director a specific rehearsal in which actors will be expected to be off-book (have their lines memorized). This may happen all at once or, more likely, in sections (one act or a couple of scenes at a time). In professional productions, scenes are typically expected to be off-book the second time they are worked on in the rehearsal room.

In the days prior to any off-book rehearsal, remind the cast (through both verbal and written reminders) of the upcoming off-book date and that they need to have all of their lines memorized by this time.

Prompting

Once a scene is off-book, a new job for the stage management team is to be on-book. This means that someone is following along word for word in the script, ready to give the next line to an actor if they become lost. This is called prompting. As trivial as this may seem, this is actually a really big responsibility—the longer a performer has to wait for their line to be delivered, the more "out of the moment" the cast becomes and the less productive the rehearsal is. It is very important to stay right on the text and jump immediately in with the line if someone calls for it. Even if it seems as though the actors know all of their lines for a scene, stick closely with the script; the moment you look away will inevitably be the moment someone forgets a line. Eliminate nearby distractions (phones, computer, etc.) to avoid becoming drawn away from the text. If there are multiple members of the stage management team, decide who will be on-book for each rehearsal and stick with the same person for that entire rehearsal block to avoid confusion. If that person needs to step away for any reason, reassign the job until they return.

Only feed a line to an actor when they call "Line." When prompting, speak clearly and loudly. Enunciate. Read them the first few words and continue the line until they begin to speak or pick it up. This will become more natural with practice and you will learn to pick up on the actors' clues as to when they need a line the more you work with them.

Sometimes an actor will take a dramatic pause within or before certain lines as part of their character choice. It can be very helpful to note these times in your script so as to avoid giving an unnecessary prompt and interrupting a theatrical moment!

Prior to reaching this rehearsal, discuss protocol with director. Some directors may want to correct the actors on incorrect line readings, even when they have not called for a line. Work out a game plan as to how this will work before starting rehearsal. Once this has been worked out, be sure to share this information with the cast and with any assistant stage managers, so that everyone is on the same page as to how rehearsal will be run.

Line Notes

Once actors are off-book, you will also need to start giving them line notes, so they know exactly which lines they need to work on. There are many different ways to take line notes, so experiment until you find a method that works best for you. Follow along closely in the script and take notes of any and all mistakes that the actor makes. Like with blocking, this is a fast-paced process so using shorthand is to your advantage. It makes the most sense to take line notes when you are running big chunks; it is, generally, unnecessary to take line notes while you are just working through scenes.

At the end of the rehearsal, line notes will need to be distributed to the actors. Some stage managers hand-write their line notes and distribute before the actors leave for the day. Others type up the notes and distribute via e-mail. If you are using a digital script you might be able to highlight, copy, and paste—depending on the program (see Appendix K). Like rehearsal reports, line notes should be issued as soon as possible after rehearsal so the actors can work on correcting their mistakes.

> To keep your script in a clean condition, put each page in a page protector and take line notes with dry or wet erase markers (wet erase markers require water to wipe off, but tend to smear less than dry erase markers). These can be easily erased at the end of every night, so that the script is clean and ready for the next run-through!

If you do not have any assistant stage managers, you will be responsible both for being on-book and for taking line notes. On-book responsibilities **always** take higher precedence than line notes or any other stage manager duties. Mark as much as you can using your shorthand as you go along, but don't fret if you miss some line mistakes. Like all aspects of stage management, this is a skill that will become easier with time and practice.

Maintaining Blocking

Once the blocking has been set, keep an eye out for consistency here as well. Just as with lines, be prepared to prompt the actors as to where their next move is if they get lost or to gently remind them of the correct blocking if they wander too far astray. For many directors, the blocking will not be set completely in stone until dress rehearsals or even opening night (with minor tweaks being made to account for spacing or lighting or the set). With this in mind, treat all blocking reminders as just that—a reminder of what was written down last time, with the knowledge that the director may prefer what the actor just made up and that the blocking may change from what is in your book.

Just as with prompting, discuss protocol with your director before rehearsals begin. Have a plan on how and when you should make comments on the blocking. (Should you interrupt the scene or let it play out and address the change when the scene is complete? Should variations be discussed with the full group or privately with the director?)

Run-Throughs

About halfway or two-thirds of the way through the rehearsal process, you will reach a point when the cast is ready to run large chunks of the show. These types of rehearsals are often referred to as "stumble-throughs" and are exactly what they sound like. The intent is to start building continuity and get a feel for the show as a whole. Blocking will be clunky, props and transitions will be forgotten, lines will be a mess, and character intricacies are often lost. However, the goal is to keep pushing forward, as much as possible, and give notes at the end. Depending on the show and the length of the rehearsal period, the stumble-through may be a small chunk of scenes, a single act, or the whole show at once.

It is nice to inform and remind the artistic staff when a run-through will take place so they can attend if they desire.

After stumble-through rehearsals, you will have at least one run-through rehearsal. Like the stumble-through, this may be taken a single act at a time or the whole show at once (again, usually dependent on the show and on your rehearsal period). By this point, the cast should have an idea of the continuity. Now the intent is to re-integrate all the things they discovered in scene rehearsals with character, as well as to have a second chance to get technical things correct (blocking, lines, prop tracking, and transitions). As with stumble-throughs, run-throughs should not stop unless absolutely necessary.

One of the run-through rehearsals (or the run-through, if there is only one) should be deemed the designer run. This will be a chance for designers to see the show before they integrate their design elements into it. Have this rehearsal on the calendar as soon as possible and send reminders about it. Before the rehearsal, provide seating for all designers. This is also a good time to get your crew in to see the show if possible. It may be the only chance they have to see a full run.

Be sure to get timings of any stumble-throughs or run-throughs. If possible, get timings not only for the whole show, but also for individual acts and scenes. At this point in the process, the specificity will assist you and the director in determining which scenes need to be tightened up. It can also be useful information to have available for your sound and lighting designers, to help with timing the length of their cues prior to tech. The front of house staff may also need this information.

As with all points in the process, the more prepared you are for these rehearsals, the smoother they will run and the less stressful it will be for all parties. Carefully track props, have a game plan for all transitions (any that are not accomplished by actors will be taken care of by you), and be ready to be glued to the book. Lines will be the first thing to slow down these rehearsals, so make sure you are not the one holding rehearsal up. These rehearsals will also be a major test of your multitasking abilities. It will be extraordinarily stressful and things will go wrong, but this is why we rehearse. You are not expected to have all the correct answers yet, or else the show would be in performances. Answer questions as best you can, take note of things that need to be solved, and remember to breathe!

Chapter Nine
Publicity

Program Information

It may be the stage manager's responsibility to compile information about the show that will be included in the printed programs. Many times, a form exists that only needs to be filled in. However, if no form exists, the form located in the appendix is a good starting point. Typical information that must be provided includes cast, crew, and designer lists, biographies (bios), headshots, time/place of the play, director's notes, length of the performance and the intermission (if there is one), special thanks, and warnings for special effects used in the production (such as fog/haze, strobe lights, smoking, strong language, etc.). For musicals, often a list of musical numbers is also requested. For information on construction crews, ask the technical director and wardrobe supervisor (see Appendix L).

Some companies, to save on printing costs, do not print bios for parts of the cast and crew; ascertain that information prior to asking for bios.

Biographies

If bios are required, ask all cast members, designers, and stage management (that includes you!) for a short bio about themselves to include in the program. Check with whoever is in charge of the program about a word limit for bios (typically around 70–100 words). Be sure to give the cast plenty of time to do these and send them constant reminders. They invariably are left until the last minute, so set an early deadline (see Appendix L.1).

Headshots

Sometimes headshots are printed in the program along with actor bios. More commonly, and especially true on Equity productions, full-sized color prints of actor headshots are mounted in the lobby for patrons to see as they arrive. Determine what will be required for the production and, just as with bios, request headshots early on and give reminders often until you have them all. Depending on the company, directors, choreographers, designers, and sometimes stage management will also be asked to provide headshots.

Special Thanks

Another very important aspect of the program is the special thanks section. Any companies, retailers, or individuals who have donated their time, skills, or products to a production should be listed in the program. Be sure to check with all designers and shop managers to get a complete list.

Publicity Photos

Sometimes, a publicity photo will be taken sometime before tech begins to help sell tickets. The date and specific photo should be chosen, taking into account what costumes and set pieces will be complete in time. As soon as possible, communicate this time and date to the production team and cast members involved in the shot. The costume designer will need to be a part of the planning so the actors can be appropriately costumed for the photo. If the location is not at the theater, make sure that it has been scheduled and/or reserved and the actors have transportation to that location. Be sure to schedule enough time for the actors to get into costume, hair, and makeup before the photographer arrives.

Interviews

Sometimes, the production company or publicist will set up interviews with the cast, designers, or director to help promote the show. This may be with a local paper, radio station, or the publicist themselves. The stage manager may be asked to help coordinate these interviews to best fit within the rehearsal schedule and the company members' availability. Additionally, with many companies the stage manager may be required to arrange transit or transport the actors themselves.

Photo Call

In most situations, it will be your responsibility to coordinate and run the photo call. Decide on a date and time as early as possible so that everyone (including actors and designers) knows when to expect it. Announce it and add it to the production calendar. About a week prior to the photo call, send an e-mail to the director and all designers (the sound designer can typically be omitted) requesting a list of the photos they would like. You should also remind the cast at this time (and again the day before). The deadline for receiving these lists should be no later than twenty-four hours before the photo call. Compile the responses and make a final list of about ten to fifteen shots (cut and combine the photos at your discretion to end up with as many different looks as you can, trying to keep as many of the photo requests as possible but also keeping the photo call to a manageable length, typically no longer than an hour).

Once you have a finalized list, go through each one and write down the setup of each photo. This includes set, props, costumes, and correct light cues, as well as which actors are in each photo. The more detailed, the better! From there, organize the photo list in the most logical possible order. Keep in mind the time it takes to do set transitions, prop reset, changing costumes/hair/makeup, etc. Copies of this list should be given to your lightboard operator, your assistant stage manager (or deck crew head), at least two for the actors (posted prominently backstage and in the dressing room), and one for yourself (see Appendix M).

> When organizing the photos, keep in mind that sometimes it is easier to move backwards through the show, rather than resetting for the top and moving forwards.

Photo calls should not last more than an hour, so plan accordingly. Also, if at all possible, take care of group photos and other full cast shots early so you can let people go as they finish (unless of course you are having a photo call before the show, then start small and work up to the full group shots). With the exception of the soundboard operator, the entire cast and crew will be required to stay throughout the length of the photo call unless personally released by the stage manager. Actors' Equity Association members have only a specific amount of time when they are allowed to be in the building and photo calls are not exempt from this time allotment.

Throughout the photo call, keep a running commentary on which shot will be taken next "on-deck" so anyone not currently participating in the shoot can be prepping backstage. Make sure any last-minute changes in the order of the photos is communicated loudly and clearly. At the end, thank everyone for their patience and participation. Be sure to do a thorough cleanup with your crew before locking up for the evening, as props and costume pieces tend to be misplaced during photo calls.

The Actors' Equity Association requires twenty-four hours' notice before any photographs may be taken, so insure proper notification of the cast takes place. Additionally, some theaters are beginning to discontinue separate photo calls. Instead a photographer will come and capture pictures during a dress rehearsal. The twenty-four-hour notification period still applies to this option.

Remember that the more prepared you come into a photo call, the less difficult it will be! Sometimes, the director, lighting designer, or even the producer will be present—do your best to find a balance of getting them what they think they need and respecting the actors' and crew's time.

Chapter Ten
Prior to Tech

Load-In

Load-in is the first day all tech elements (lights, set, and sound) will be brought into the theater. In some theaters that is the first time any technical element will be allowed in the theater. This typically takes place a couple of days before the first tech rehearsal. It will be your chance to prepare the space for the actors. This is usually the point at which you will receive keys for the theater.

Take this time to become very familiar with the space; find all bathrooms, water fountains, and the callboard (or a good central place to put a makeshift callboard), familiarize yourself with the booth and the place you'll be stationed to call cues, and find a prop table and a good location for it backstage. Explore all paths through the theater. Try to get lost (if you can, the actors are bound to) and, if you do, figure out how to get back. Start planning out where you are going to need run lights (for safe passage, seeing prop tables, and having quick changes); identify what might be a safety hazard, and which doors lock automatically (these will need to be taped open during the show if there is any possibility of them being used), including doors that will be accessed during smoke breaks.

Once you feel good about the space, get to work on organizing the backstage in the best orientation for your show's needs and finalizing your show paperwork.

Preset Checklist

One of the pre-tech tasks is to compile a preset list. This should include all set pieces and props that need to be set onstage/backstage prior to the start of the show, as well as any other preshow duties (sweeping, turning off work lights, washing dishes, etc.). This should also include any costumes that need to be specially set backstage or onstage. Copies of this should be given to your assistant stage manager(s) and a copy should be kept in the promptbook. Next to each item, it can be helpful to have a column for each dress rehearsal and performance so they can be checked off before each run. Post a copy of the preset list on the callboard or other central location. This list will evolve throughout tech week, but coming in with a preliminary list will make tech run more smoothly (see Appendix N).

Run Sheets

A run sheet lists all the transitions that happen in the show. This includes all set changes (including flies and automation), prop movement (backstage or on/offstage), and costume quick changes—anything technical that the crew or cast has to do during the run of the show.

Start by listing each scene. Fill in basic information for the transitions between the scenes (scene changes). This is where the post-it notes that you have been keeping during rehearsals will come in handy! Go through scene by scene and track all of the props as they move on or offstage, and note where they enter/exit and who will be moving them. When these are not assigned to specific actors, assign crew members to them. For scene changes, assign crew/available cast members to move set pieces and set props, and help with costume quick changes.

Prior to making your run sheets, have a discussion with the director about who (actors or crew members or both) will be doing scene changes. Depending on the budget of the production as well as the esthetic the director is going for, they may want the actors to perform all of the transitions or not be a part of them at all. This information will also need to be taken into consideration when hiring the stage crew so that the correct number of crew are brought onboard for the show.

Print multiple copies. Give a copy to your assistant stage manager(s) and post copies in multiple places backstage. If the resources are available, have physical copies for each crew member as well.

> When posted backstage, always place these lists by a run light so that they can be easily viewed.

This way, they can take personal notes on their specific jobs. It is a good idea to keep electronic versions of all paperwork. Keep a copy on a personal computer as well as additional backup copies in multiple locations (flash drives, cloud-based storage, etc.) (see Appendix O).

Take time before the first tech rehearsal to go over the run sheets with everyone who has an assignment. Make sure they know what they are moving, when they move it, how it moves, and where they are expected to move it.

It is very important to keep the run sheets updated, as things change throughout the rehearsal process. Ask the crew to make notes on the run sheets, collect the run sheets at the end of rehearsals, make the changes, and print new copies before the next rehearsal. Accuracy is important as well. Should any member of the crew call in sick, their job should be documented well enough that the show can be run seamlessly by a stand-in.

Postshow Lists

Next to the preset list, there should also be a postshow checklist. This lists everything that has to happen before everyone leaves for the night. Make sure it is clear that these items are just as important to get done as the preset items and that no one on the stage management team should leave the building until the list is complete (this could include locking up weapons, cleaning up food or fake blood, getting furniture out of the way if there is a day crew, etc.) (see Appendix P).

> Go over all backstage paperwork with the assistant stage manager or deck crew head. Be thorough to make sure that they know what is required of them. Ask if they have any questions and make sure that they know to communicate an issue if anything comes up.

Prepping the Stage and Backstage

Transferring Spike Marks

When it is time to move from the rehearsal space to the performance space, measure the locations of any spike marks for furniture or scenery that were not originally on the groundplan or that have been modified during rehearsal. Plot those points exactly as was done for the original tape out so they can be easily transferred to the theater.

If rehearsals are taking place on the performance stage or if spike marks are transferred before the floor treatment has been completed, be sure to take precautions before any paint covers up your marks. Keep open communication with the scenic designer and scenic painter about when the floor treatment will be happening and schedule time prior to that to cover up your spike marks—1-inch masking or blue painter's tape works very well for this. Tape over your spike marks, being careful to cover your full mark but as little of the stage as possible. Leave a little "flag" in the painter's tape (a small folded-over section that makes the tape easier to grasp and pull up). After painting is complete, simply go back through and peel up the masking tape, leaving your spike mark (and its color!) intact.

Once spike marks are final (they have been transferred onto the performance stage, spacing has been finalized, and all floor treatments are complete), it is a good idea to cover them with clear vinyl (Marley) tape. This type of tape is manufactured to seam dance floors, but can come in handy to help secure spike marks and dance numbers. This will prevent the tape from pulling up over the course of performances. If Marley tape is not available, clear packing tape works as well, although it is not as durable or long lasting.

Adding Safety Tape

An important step before and during tech rehearsals is to lay down safety tape in any areas of the stage (either onstage or behind the set) where actors will be moving that may pose a safety threat (e.g., stairs, ledges, masking flats) (see Figure 10.1). Sometimes white gaff tape is all that is needed, other times glow tape may be required. White gaff tape works better in very low light situations, while glow tape works best in total darkness. Glow tape is specialized tape coated with photo-luminescent pigments that absorb and store energy from ambient light. In a blackout, the tape glows, allowing actors to see without needing to wait for their eyes to adjust. A great tool, but, just as with all specialized theatrical tape, it is expensive so use thoughtfully; a small amount can go a long way. Glow gaff tape also exists; it is just as expensive but can be ripped by hand. Ultimately, it is important that the actors are safe no matter the cost of tape, so take the necessary precautions to insure their safety.

Clearing Actor Pathways

Another step in insuring safety backstage is to leave clear pathways to all areas on and offstage where actors must travel. Areas should be swept or vacuumed where possible (especially quick change areas where actors may be in bare feet) and be free of any trip hazards. Any cables crossing these paths must be either taped down or covered with carpet (this is usually addressed by the electricians, but it never hurts to keep an extra eye out for stray cables!). Any screws or other metal snags sticking out of walls or floors should be removed or covered with tape to avoid scrapes or ripped costumes. Wherever possible, pathways should be lit with run lights.

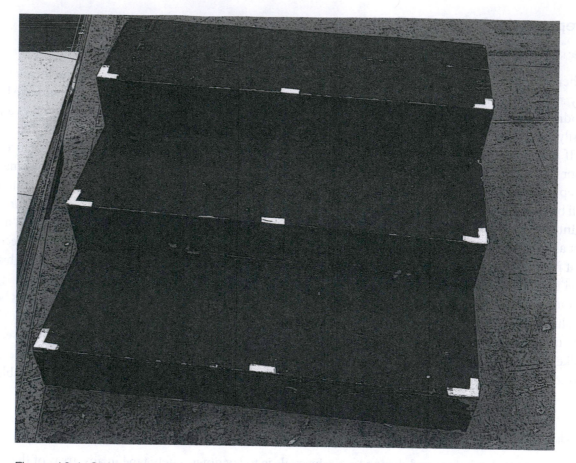

Figure 10.1 Safety Tape Example

Glow Spikes

Depending on the show, some spike marks may need glow tape in order to be found in the dark. Ask the actors if there are any particular trouble areas that they would like to be glow taped. If actors are going to need to exit in a blackout, a path of glow tape may need to be created for them. Confer with the scenic and lighting designers to insure that the glow tape is minimally intrusive to the design. Again though, safety first.

It is a good idea to keep at least one flashlight backstage, both for emergency safety reasons and to "charge" any glow tape that doesn't get light exposure during the run of the show. This is a good task to include on the preshow checklist or run sheet.

Run Lights

Run lights are colored light bulbs or dark-gelled lights (traditionally blue) used to help ease navigation backstage in the dark during performances. Depending on where quick changes are taking place, run lights may need to be added so the wardrobe crew can see to complete the change. They are typically either clip lights plugged into the wall or stage lights controlled by the lightboard (and programmed to be on throughout the run). The lights are usually provided and hung by the lighting department (under the advisement of stage management for location). Add it to the preshow/postshow checklists to turn them on and off before/after each performance (if not board controlled).

Prop Tables

Part of preshow setup includes presetting props backstage. For this, acquire or designate a table/flat surface as the props table (you may want one for each side of the stage or strategically placed near the various entrances to the stage, depending on the theater). Prior to the start of each tech rehearsal and performance, have all actors check their personal props to make sure that they are preset in the correct location. The prop table should have its own run light so it can be utilized during the show. A good way to organize props is to tape out and label a specific area for each prop on the table. This way, props can be easily found and also can be quickly identified if missing. This can also be done with butcher paper and a marker (see Figures 10.2 a and b).

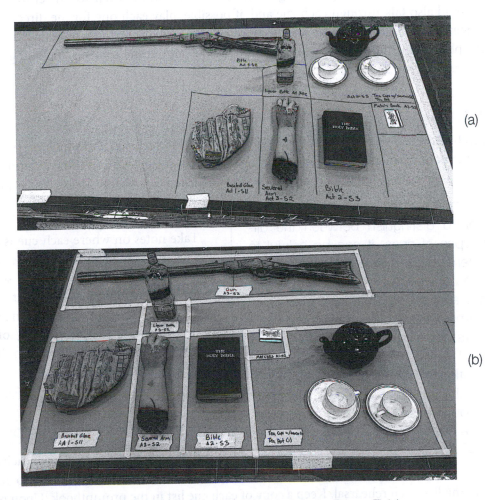

(a)

(b)

Figure 10.2 a. Props Table Labeled with Marker, b. Props Table Labeled with Tape

Be sure to print a complete and finalized prop list and keep it near either the props table or prop storage for quick reference.

Paper Tech and Dry Tech

Prior to the first tech rehearsal, it is important to have either a paper tech and/or a dry tech. These are rehearsals involving only the director, the stage manager, the light designer, and the sound designer. The scenic designer, music director, choreographer, wardrobe supervisor, and costume designer may also be present for a scenic or costume heavy show with shifts or quick changes.

Paper Tech

For many productions, only a paper tech is necessary. Paper techs are held as a meeting, rather than a rehearsal, and cues are talked through, rather than fully presented. The light designer should give a basic overview of each look so the stage manager and the director know what to expect to see. The sound designer should also talk through each cue and, if possible, play each one for the director to hear. The stage manager is in charge of running this meeting. Talk through the script in order and take notes about cue names, placement, and intent. Also talk through how large scene changes, including flies, will take place (go over your run sheet).

Dry Tech

On technical-heavy shows, a dry tech may be necessary. This is a rehearsal in which everyone except the cast sits in the performance space and goes through the show cue by cue and (if necessary) scene shift by scene shift. This gives the director a chance to look at and listen to each cue. It also allows the stage manager to become familiar with the cues and where they will be called.

In order to distinguish between the different types of cues, it can be helpful to label them using different systems (e.g., light cues are numbered, sound cues are lettered, and scene shifts are given creative names). Be sure to consult with your designers when coming up with a labeling system. This will help with quick and easy identification with the crew and over headset. Just be sure that whatever system or theme you use isn't confusing or misleading to the crew.

Take notes on where each cue is in the script and when it should be called. Write a one-to-two-word description of the look and sound of each cue (e.g., scene light up). Once performances are underway, it will be the stage manager's responsibility to maintain the integrity of these cues for the designers, so it is important for you to be familiar with them.

Prepping the Calling Script

You should have cue lists from each designer by this time. If one hasn't been provided, request one prior to the first tech rehearsal. Keep a copy of each cue list in the promptbook. Upon receiving the cue lists, add all cues to the calling script. WRITE IN PENCIL. Draw a line in the margin next to the line or place in the script where the cue will be called. Write on the line what type of cue it is and the cue number (e.g., light cue number 42 would be written LQ42 or LX42. Sound cues are often written with the shorthand FX or SQ and named using letters). Also on this line, include a brief description of the cue to serve as a reminder to their purpose (e.g., "daytime look," "doorbell," "transition music," "blackout"). Indicate in the script exactly where you will be calling the cue as well. Underline, highlight (only for final placements), or box the cue-word/line. If the cue is taken off a visual or an audio cue, specify the timing in a consistent location near the listed cue.

If you haven't already, add the scene shifts from the run sheet into your book. The two things you need to note are, what signals the start of the scene shift (light cue, sound cue, stage manager called cue, or actor driven cue), and how you will know the shift is complete and that the following scene can begin (a visual cue, or a confirmation from the deck chief or assistant stage manager over headset). It can also be helpful to include details about the scene shift—who is involved, what each person is responsible for doing, and the order of the scene shift (e.g., the table must go offstage before the tree flies in). Be sure to get confirmation of any offstage shifts that you are unable to see with your own eyes (quick costume changes, mic swaps, etc.).

The final step is to add standbys. About half a page prior to a cue, a standby will need to be called to the board ops and crew members. Write these standbys in your calling script so that you remember to call them. These will be beneficial to avoid ever being surprised by a cue and to make sure everyone is prepared for the cue, change, or shift. When multiple cues occur in close succession, a single standby can be given as prep ("Standby light Qs 9 thru 11"). Standbys that include a shift should be given with enough time for people to get to their assigned positions for the shift (assume they are in the green room or on the wrong side of the stage) (see Appendix Q).

Take the time to make the calling script as neat, precise, and detailed as possible. Ask designers for cue lists as soon as possible so you have time to ask questions, clarify call timing, and get it all down in the calling script. Not only will it make calling the show much easier and less stressful, but it will also guarantee an accurate and consistent show. This is critical not only for the safety of the performers and the company, but also for maintaining the artistic integrity of the light, sound, scenic, and costume designs. Calling a cue inaccurately is the same as an actor paraphrasing their lines. The general gist is simply not good enough. Just as an actor must strive to be word perfect, the stage manager must strive to be cue perfect.

Be sure that anything written is large and legible enough to be seen clearly and easily under blue run lights. Feel free to color code as long as your colors will not be adversely affected by blue light. Be cautious using stickers, flags, and sticky notes, as they can fall off, move, or tear your pages, especially during long-running productions. If you are creating a digital version, make sure it is easily legible and that the fonts are easily distinguishable.

First Day Onstage

The first time the actors move into the theater, set time aside right at the start of rehearsal to give a tour of the space. Point out bathrooms, dressing rooms, the green room, and pathways backstage. Now is the time to fill the cast in on any important information about the theater (food/drink rules, quirky theater features, potential safety hazards, etc.). This is also a chance for the designers to say a few words (especially the costume, wig, and/or makeup designers who will be working most directly with the actors in the coming tech rehearsals).

If the cast has never rehearsed on the stage before, a spacing rehearsal may be scheduled. This rehearsal is a time to walk through the blocking, and allow the director to see it in the actual performance space and make adjustments as needed. Depending on the timeline, this spacing rehearsal may cover the entire show or only potentially problematic scenes (scenes with particularly complex blocking, large group scenes, or scenes where exact placement of actors is essential). Determine if the designers or technical director need to be present to help familiarize the stage manager with any technical elements.

Last Rehearsal Before Tech

At the end of your last rehearsal before tech, take a moment to let the actors know what to expect in the upcoming rehearsals.

- Remind the cast not to wear white or bright clothing for tech rehearsals for lighting purposes. The lighting designer may even request that actors wear colors similar to their costumes—check with them prior to this discussion so as to give the cast accurate instructions.
- Let them know that things are still being finalized. They should let you know if something is missing, broken, or problematic, but they shouldn't expect it to appear or be fixed right away.
- Remind them to get plenty of rest and drink lots of water.
- It is also a good time to gently remind them that tech will be less focused on them than the preceding rehearsal process.

You should also have another moment with your director about their expectations regarding tech. It can be helpful to set goals about where you would like to end each day of tech.

Crew Calls

Once you have a good grasp on the preshow checklist and the amount of resetting the crew will need to do each day, you should figure out call times. Some theaters have set call times and IATSE (the stage-hands union) has specific rules about when you can be in the space. If there isn't a standard or manda-tory call, a good rule of thumb is to call the deck crew one hour before half hour (ninety minutes before curtain). For rehearsals, you can usually get away with just a half hour before the actor call (this actually gives them an hour assuming that the actors will take half an hour). Of course, if the prop list is twenty pages long it might take them a bit longer to check, so make your best estimate and adjust as you go.

Depending on the complexity of the light plot, the person doing dimmer check (sometimes the board op, sometimes the master electrician) should be in half an hour before the crew (two hours before curtain). This gives them time to troubleshoot if anything goes wrong.

The sound operator will need time to prep and check all of the mics and speakers, and to troubleshoot things if necessary. If you are responsible for determining their call time, start them at the same time as the deck crew.

Investing in Blacks

Early in the process, be sure to mention that all backstage crew (including assistant stage managers) will be required to wear all black for all dress rehearsals and performances. This entails long black pants, long- and short-sleeved shirts (can be short sleeves for warm-weather shows and shows in which you don't appear onstage for scene changes; short sleeves plus a long-sleeved hoodie/sweatshirt is also acceptable), and black close-toed shoes. For some productions, the crew that appear onstage will be costumed to fit into the world of the play, rather than in black. If this is the case, schedule fittings with the wardrobe supervisor and each crew member. Also make sure that your costume designer knows this as early as possible.

Just as backstage crew must dress appropriately, it is equally important for the stage manager to wear rehearsal- and performance-appropriate outfits. It can be fun to dress up, especially for opening nights, but be sure to always have comfortable, close-toed shoes (no heels, ladies!) and clothing with pockets (belt loops can also be very useful for clipping on headsets, etc.). Be prepared to have a situation come up where you may need to paint something, use a power tool, carry heavy objects throughout the building, climb around in the grid, or anything else imaginable that may need to be resolved at the last moment. Functionality is top priority. In terms of colors, this varies from theater to theater and event to event. Blacks may not be necessary, especially if you are never seen by the audience, but typically dark tones are preferable. Additionally, if you wear black, it can be seen as a sign of solidarity with the crew.

Chapter Eleven
Tech Rehearsals

Once it gets into tech rehearsals, the show becomes the responsibility of the stage manager. From this point on, the stage manager runs all rehearsals and performances and it is their job to maintain the integrity of the show as the director intended.

Begin tech rehearsals by talking with the cast and crew and explaining how the tech rehearsal process will run. Make sure that it is clear that stage management is running the rehearsal. This information can come from either the director or directly from management (the technical director or production manager may run this discussion—touch base with them and find out). Remind the cast (and the director) that this is purely a rehearsal for the technical elements. They should not be taking time to work on acting moments during this rehearsal, unless they directly impact technical elements. Above all, the actors should be watching out for their safety during these rehearsals (getting used to being on the set, working with the lights and sound, etc.). Have them keep an eye out for dangerous locations backstage/onstage that need more glow tape or need a run light and inform them that if at any time during the rehearsal they feel like they are in immediate danger, they should call "Hold!" so the problem can be addressed and resolved. If they feel unsafe but it is not an immediate safety concern, ask them to notify stage management at the next break. Finally, thank them in advance for their patience and cooperation. Tech rehearsals can be very stressful and confusing and also can get very boring for the actors. The more cooperation you can get from them, the faster and more smoothly the whole process will go.

Types of Tech Rehearsals

The first tech rehearsal can be run one of two ways: either a cue-to-cue can take place or a full tech run. Discuss this with the director and technical director prior to tech rehearsal. This is a decision that will likely be made after paper/dry tech. If the first tech rehearsal is also first rehearsal on stage, the rehearsal will often serve as a staging rehearsal as well.

Cue-to-cue

In a cue-to-cue rehearsal, the show is run through in order, skipping, just as the name suggests, from cue to cue. These rehearsals are more common in straight plays and shows with minimal cues. In a musical or other heavily cued show, where cues are frequent and rely heavily on precise timing, a Stop and Start Rehearsal is much more beneficial.

The best way to run a cue-to-cue is to have the actors begin a few lines before the cue so that a standby can be given, run through the cue, and then slightly beyond the cue to give the director a chance to look at the cue and for the stage manager to make sure the cue was called correctly. (For details on how to call cues, see Calling Cues). Once you have run the scene beyond the cue, call "Hold, please!" Always insure the cue fade has completed before calling hold; sometimes fades are longer and need twenty to thirty seconds or longer to complete. If the cue or sequence of cues needs to be re-run, have everyone reset and repeat the cue. If everything went smoothly, then find the next place in the script and tell the cast, "We will be skipping ahead to . . ." Make sure both the cast and crew know to wait for a specific "GO" from the stage manager before beginning the new section. This allows the stage manager to communicate with all necessary parties before beginning. If there are multiple cues in sequence or if the next upcoming cue is less than a page from the previous, have the actors continue to run the scene through to the next cue rather than stopping and skipping ahead.

When trying to decide if it is time to skip ahead, the stage manager should use their best judgment of how much time it takes to reset versus just continuing to play the scene. Generally speaking if it is less than a page, just keep going.

Start and Stop Rehearsal

A start and stop rehearsal is similar to a cue-to-cue in that it is meant to acquaint everyone with the technical elements of the show and allow the stage manager time to learn the correct placement of all the cues. These are typical for shows that are heavily cued, like musicals, so rather than skipping from cue to cue, this type of rehearsal runs through the majority of the show—starting, stopping, resetting, and rerunning as necessary until everyone understands what needs to happen. If there is a large section of text without any cues, it may be skipped over.

These rehearsals are a chance to get the timing down for calling the cues and for the board ops/run crew to become familiar with their jobs, so take the time to make sure everyone feels confident in what they are doing. This time is specifically for everyone to practice the transitions and cues; it's okay to rerun things, just make sure to keep within the allotted time slot(s).

Full Tech Run

Once a cue-to-cue or start and stop has been completed (or, if the show is simple enough that it doesn't require a cue-to-cue), a full tech run will take place. This is a full run-through of the show in which all of the technical elements (sans costumes) are integrated. The goal is typically to try to do a full run without stopping. However, at these rehearsals it is absolutely okay to call "Hold!" and go back to fix or re-run a cue if necessary. This is the time to work out kinks and figure out timing so that by the time dress rehearsals are reached, a full run can take place without stopping for technical issues.

Headsets

In many theaters, once it is time for tech rehearsals and performances, headsets will be used to communicate between all crew members. The type of headset will depend greatly on the theater. It is important to familiarize yourself with how the system functions. If it is a wired system (cords connect the units to the wall), make sure that the crew will be able to perform their duties or reach the locations they need to reach while on headset. If headsets are unavailable, determine how communication between the booth and backstage will take place. In some theaters, different communication systems may exist for front of house and backstage (e.g., walkie-talkies for front of house and headsets for backstage).

Headset Protocol

Keep non-show chatter to a minimum (so as not to miss cues or take up the communication line in case of an emergency). Never talk during a standby or calling sequence. Be conscientious of the topics discussed as well; some green rooms or box offices have a monitor station and can hear anything said over headset.

Prior to tech rehearsals, discuss headset protocol with the crew. Do you want them to let you know they are on headset? Let them know your preference of response to a standby (standing by, copy, "name of assignment," etc.). Do you want them to respond to the standby in a specific order? Remind them about chatter. Make sure they know how to use the headset and won't inadvertently leave their channel open, thus causing unnecessary noise or a block in communication. If you are using wireless headsets, make sure that they know how to prep and strike them each day (or charge the walkie-talkies, etc.). Make sure they know not to say "Go" or anything sounding like it with their com open. If for some reason they need to get off headset, they should let you know when they leave and when they return, but they should make sure you aren't in the middle of a standby or calling sequence. Let them know that if you say "Clear on headset" it means stop talking immediately and wait until you are finished; you can also use "You're clear" to let them know they are okay to talk (avoid saying "Go ahead").

Who's on Headset (Typically)

During Tech

Stage manager, assistant stage manager(s), deck chief, flyrail, automation, board ops, deck crew (optional), programmers (optional), lighting designer, sound designer (optional). Ask the designers for their preference. Headsets may come from sound, electrics, or production - find out who is responsible well in advance of tech.

During Dress/Shows

Stage manager, assistant stage manager(s), board ops, house manager, deck crew (optional).

A God mic is a microphone dedicated to the stage manager to allow them to communicate with the cast and crew, call holds, and give instructions. Make sure to ask the technical director or sound engineer about the possibility of having a God mic; it will save your voice over a long tech period. And if you are lucky, it will go through the green room and dressing room monitors as well!

Calling Cues

The stage manager's job during the run of the show is to orchestrate the performance to make sure everything runs smoothly and consistently. A significant component of this is calling the cues. For the dress rehearsals and performances, you will be up in the booth or backstage (depending on the venue and preference) calling cues as you watch the performance.

By this point, you will have written all of the cues in your script, as well as the standbys. To call a cue, announce a standby to all parties affected by the cue (usually over headset) about fifteen to thirty seconds prior to the cue, then call the cue number and "GO."

"Standby Light cue 43"
(Fifteen to thirty seconds elapsed time)
"Cue 43 . . . GO"

Cues that happen simultaneously or in very close succession should be given a single standby ("Standby Lights 25 through 29, Sound O, and scene change "crimson").

It is extremely important for you to call all cues clearly and calmly so that there is no confusion. It can be beneficial to request confirmation from your crews on standby calls, just so you know that they have heard the call and are ready to go. Instruct them to respond to a standby with "Standing by." Sometimes, however, there will not be enough time between the standby and the cue or else giving confirmation may tie up the headsets for too long, so use this system at your own discretion.

As you rehearse, you will become more familiar with the cues and it will be easier to call them more accurately. Don't get frustrated if you don't do it right the first time! Also remember that with live theatre, every performance is different. You may have to adjust some calls nightly depending on audience reactions, delays backstage, etc. The important thing is to remain alert and constantly ready to adapt.

The "G-O" word should never be said over headset unless an actual call is being made, and no one should ever say "GO" over headset except the stage manager. It sounds silly, but spell it out unless actually calling a cue. It is also helpful to avoid words that might sound like "GO."

There is a video called Standby Cue 101, which serves as a very helpful guide for first-time stage managers. This video should answer most of your questions regarding how to call cues.

Quick Change Rehearsals

Just as scene changes must be choreographed and practiced with the stage crew, complicated and/or fast costume changes (also known as quick changes) must also be choreographed and practiced with the actors and wardrobe crew (or whoever is executing the change). If the costume is ready to be worked with, these quick change rehearsals will take place during tech rehearsals. If not, time should be set aside during the first dress rehearsal to practice.

Locations backstage should be designated for each quick change. They should be located near a light source (either in the green room, dressing room, under a run light, or in an area with consistent light leak from the stage). All actors and crew should be made aware of when and where each quick change takes place so they can stay out of the way unless involved. Whenever possible and depending on the nature of the costume change, equip the quick change area with a mirror, clothing hook, and a table or chair to preset the costume. Assign a crew or fellow cast member to assist with the change and give all involved a chance to talk with the costume designer to determine the best way to execute the change. Once a plan is in place, run the change as it will happen during the show with as accurate timing as possible. Reset and give them a chance to run it again, either to adjust their plan or to solidify the one they have. Encourage them to rehearse it during downtime.

Chapter Twelve
Dress Rehearsals

Dress rehearsals should be run as though they were performances. All possible final aspects of the show should be in place and actors and crew should act as though there is an audience in the house. At this point, actors should no longer be sitting in the house during the run. Actors should be in full costume and crew should be in blacks or costume. Since many times this is the first run with costumes, holds may need to be called for changes that cannot be made, but when possible, avoiding holds is preferable. Depending on the complexity of the change and its impact on the timing of transitions, you may run a few of the costume changes before the first dress rehearsal.

Management should arrive in time to completely prep the performance space. This call time will vary depending on the preset list and how long it takes to get prepped. Plan for at least forty-five minutes to start.

Preshow Setup (Checks)

Preshow for the stage management team means insuring that all aspects of the production are in their proper place, on, and functioning for the run of the show. Just as during rehearsals, stage management arrives first to unlock doors and turn on lights. Next, the stage must be swept and/or mopped in preparation for preset. By this point, the crew has arrived and preset can begin. In accordance with the preset checklists, each crew member should be tasked with specific assignments that they complete for each show so that nothing gets missed (see Appendix N.1). During this time, the stage manager will prepare their own area, insuring that their promptbook is open and ready, that all cue lights work, and headsets and monitors are on and functioning. If the show has minimal or no crew, the stage management team will be responsible for all preset tasks.

Once all scenic elements are in place, props have been set (both onstage and off), and quick change costumes have been set, stage management (or the stage manager and a crew member, if there are no assistant stage managers on the production) will perform "checks." This means to walk the set with preset list in hand, checking that every element of the show is in its correct place for the start of the show. By doing checks with two people, one can read off the preset list while the second can put eyes on each item and verbally verify that it is accounted for. This greatly reduces the chance for something to be missed or skipped over. The house cannot be opened until checks have taken place.

Time Checks

The stage management team will be relied upon to keep track of time for the performers, crew, house manager, and audience members. As stage manager, it is your job to keep careful track of what time it is and call warning times backstage. Either in person or over a headset, call out the amount of time and what the countdown is to (e.g., "Five minutes to warm-ups!" "Ten minutes to house open," or "Places!"). When a time is called, it is up to the stage management team to relay this information to everyone else. When receiving a time call, it is proper etiquette to respond with "Thank you ____" ("Thank you places," "Thank you ten," etc.). This confirms that they have received the information. Maintaining this communication backstage is very important, so don't slack in this regard! The actors, crew, and front of house need to know the time calls in order to properly gage their preparation. It is up to you what you count down to, but be consistent (some people call "To places" while others call "To curtain," etc.). Typical calls are half hour, fifteen minutes, and five minutes.

Mic Checks

If microphones are used during a show, typically time must be set aside before the house opens for mic checks. These should happen as soon after the actors arrive as possible to allow time for any troubleshooting. The sound technician should arrive with enough time to get all mics prepped before the actors arrive. Have actors put on their makeup and then their mic (to avoid getting any makeup in the mic) and send them onstage for mic checks. Prior to the first use of mics, have the technical director or sound technician give a tutorial to all actors on proper mic handling to avoid any damage to the units. It is important that actors do not reposition their mics after the sound/mic check.

Fight/Dance Call

If the show involves any fights, you will need to have a daily fight call. This should take place ten to fifteen minutes prior to the full actor call time (depending on how much time you need to run fights) and will be supervised by yourself and the fight captain (a cast member chosen by the fight choreographer). Run through all fights as instructed by your fight choreographer, making sure everything runs safely and smoothly. For safety, there should be silence apart from any noise from the fighting actors during the fight call. Fight calls typically are at half speed for the first run-through. If everyone involved feels comfortable, then the speed can be ramped up to three-quarter speed, which is usually the fastest you will ever run a fight, even in a performance.

An early call can also be given to complicated dances or choreography. For this, call all actors who are involved in the number, as well as the dance captain (again, a cast member chosen by the choreographer), ten to fifteen minutes prior to the full actor call time.

Sound/Light Check

Prior to opening the house for each performance, the board operators should run light and sound checks. The designers should instruct them on how to do this during tech rehearsals. This is to make sure that the sound cues are functioning and that levels are correct. It also checks that all lighting instruments are functioning and that the focus hasn't changed. This can be the stage manager's job if they are also acting as a board operator.

Actor Notes

Following all dress rehearsals, the director will likely gather all the actors to the stage or to the house to give notes. Typically, actors are given five to ten minutes to get out of costume and grab something on which to write notes. Keep careful track of this time and gather everyone as quickly as possible so as to release them at a reasonable time once notes have been given. Stay and listen to this notes session, both to keep it efficient and also to gather any notes that may apply to you or the crew. Quiet postshow cleanup and shutdown can take place during these notes as long as it is not distracting to the actors and director.

Tech Notes

Just as with the actors, tech notes will also be given after each tech/dress rehearsal. Make sure that all crew heads, designers, directors, and any other personnel requested by the director stick around after the run to get notes. These commonly take place after actor notes; however, if possible suggest to the director that while actors are getting out of costume and makeup tech notes could be given and allow the designers to take action sooner. Take notes during this discussion and include them in the rehearsal report.

Postshow Cleanup

After each run of the show, everything must be cleaned up and put away for storage until the next show. Collect all props (especially personal props, which tend to walk away in actor pockets or be hidden in costumes), turn off all lighting, sound, and projection equipment, including monitors, collect microphones, and clean the stage of any spills or messes that may take place in the show. Dishes should be washed and any edibles must be disposed of or refrigerated if necessary. Just as with preset, assign specific tasks to each crew member that they will be responsible for throughout the run of the production so that nothing is overlooked. Use a checklist similar to the preshow list to insure that all tasks are complete. Once everything is complete and everyone is out of the building, turn off the lights and lock up.

Chapter Thirteen
Prior to Opening Night

Looking Ahead

When everything has been made performance ready, it is time to start thinking about the run of the show. Once the show opens, the artistic integrity of the director, choreographer, and all the designers will be in your hands. As intimidating as this may sound, it will be easy as long as you plan ahead and communicate with each person before they leave. In the days leading up to opening night, plan on meeting one-on-one with each designer and technical director to discuss the protocol for anything that may happen during the run of the show and whose responsibility the notes will be. Make sure to include this in a report so everyone is on the same page.

Costumes

The most prominent upkeep for this department will be laundry. Discuss with your costume designer which pieces will need to be laundered and how (as well as how often), which should be vodka-sprayed, and which should be dry cleaned. Laundry duty will fall either to stage management or to the wardrobe crew, depending on the production. If laundry facilities are not available in the theater, come up with a plan on where it will be done, as well as a budget and method of payment (petty cash, reimbursement, etc.). Put together a laundry schedule so that all laundry is complete and dry before the next performance.

Vodka Water: this is just a simple mixture of vodka and water in a spray bottle that helps keep items sanitized and smelling decent without needing a full wash. It is often used on difficult-to-wash costumes and cuts down on dry cleaning costs. Some theaters or academic settings may not be allowed to purchase or have vodka on the premises, in which case Febreeze or Lysol spray may be used. Be aware of sensitivities or allergies to these chemicals.

The other item to discuss with this department is repairs. Decide who is responsible for minor repairs and who should be contacted to take care of any major repairs/damage. It is extremely beneficial for you or another member of the stage management team to be proficient in hand sewing to take care of minor repairs or for emergency fixes mid-show. Ask the costume designer to leave a basic repair kit backstage that includes a variety of needles, thread that matches the costumes, extra buttons, snaps, hooks, and safety pins. If renting costumes, get a rundown of what can be done to the clothing and always ask before doing any repairs yourself.

> Never wash anything that is dry clean only or vintage unless specific instructions have been given, no matter what has happened to it. Arrange for emergency dry cleaning if necessary.

Scenic

Repairs and general maintenance are the big things to be prepared for in this department. Have the scenic designer and technical director walk you through the entire set and point out areas to keep an eye on through the run of the show. Be sure to have a good working knowledge of anything that moves, flies, rolls, or has potential to cause injury. Make sure that you have access to a basic set of tools (power drill, screws, hammer, staple gun, etc.) and paint for any touch-ups. Finally, discuss cleaning protocol for the set: what should be swept, mopped, vacuumed? How often?

Props

Props tend to break, go missing, or run out. While preventing the first two items on that list will fall primarily to your assistant stage managers or deck crew head, it's important to keep an eye on all three. Keep particularly close watch on items that are rented or borrowed, as these need to be returned in good condition once the show closes. This is where keeping a carefully organized prop table is to your advantage. For expendable items, make a plan with your props master on how these are to be maintained. Take note of where and how replacement/refill items can be obtained, how often edibles need to be replaced, recipes for colored liquids, etc. Additionally, determine who is responsible for obtaining replacement items once the show opens, what the budget is, and how payments should be made (petty cash, reimbursement, etc.).

On any shows with weaponry, get in-depth training on how to properly handle, maintain, clean, and store all pieces. This information may come from the props master or from the fight choreographer. The fight captain should also be present for this discussion.

Lights

Much of light maintenance will probably fall to your board operator or master electrician. However, you should make a point to familiarize yourself with the light system, the plot, and the equipment being used. Have the lighting designer show you the location of the dimmer rack, lighting storage (for replacement lamps, gels, etc. in case of burn outs), run you through channel check, and show you the basic focus of the lights. Ask if there are particular instruments to watch out for: lights located on booms or on the floor that are likely to be kicked or bumped out of focus. If there is haze or fog being used, have them show you where it is located and what to watch out for if something malfunctions. Additionally, have a plan in place for what to do if you run out of fluid and add monitoring the fluid levels to your preshow checklist.

Sound

Like lights, sound maintenance will also likely be taken care of primarily by the board operator. Sit down with the sound designer and make sure you know the plan for sound check and if there are any cues you should be keeping a special ear out for. If microphones are being used, familiarize yourself (and at least one assistant stage manager or backstage crew member) with basic troubleshooting should anything come up pre- or mid-show (know how to change a battery, replace an element, switch frequencies, and where mic tape should go). Monitor the supplies for microphones as well: batteries, condoms (commonly used to help protect body mic packs from sweaty actors; if it falls to you to replace them, make sure you get un-lubricated), and mic tape. If mic belts are being used, consider throwing them in the laundry once or twice a week as well. If spare microphones exist, know where they are stored and how to put them into service if needed.

Direction, Choreography, and Vocals

In addition to technical maintenance, the directors will all be relying on you to maintain the show as they shaped it during rehearsals. At this point, you will likely be well acquainted with the commonly missed lines, the actor that likes to make up his blocking, the dance break that never quite got enough rehearsal time, and the harmonies that sometimes give you goosebumps but other times sound like dying cats. These you will know to watch out for, but take the time to sit down with each director (stage, music, choreography, and fight) and talk through what they would like you to look for. The performance will evolve and reshape itself slightly throughout the performances, especially in long-running productions as the actors discover and rediscover the play, and this is okay as long as it maintains the intentions of the directors. If things begin to vary too much from the original show, take note and inform the appropriate director of the change. Leave it to them to decide what action they would like you to take to address the issue.

Stage Management

Now that everything has been finalized, take the time to insure that all paperwork within your promptbook is up to date, clean, and legible. All finalized run sheets from crew members (including wardrobe) should be submitted to you prior to opening night so copies can be made and kept in the promptbook throughout the run. If anyone is ever out sick or has an emergency, the person covering their track has an accurate and reliable list to work off.

If you take these basic steps before opening, you will be much more prepared to maintain the show. More than anything, trust your instincts. You know this show better than anyone in the room, so you will be able to detect if anything goes wrong. Include any and all notes in the performance report (see Chapter 14—Performance Report) so that designers can decide if further action is required for any given mishap. And, when in doubt, ask!

Chapter Fourteen
Performances

Front of House

Front of house refers to the lobby area (box office, concession stand, etc.) and to the personnel who attend to these areas. *House* can also be in reference to the seating area of the theater or the audience.

House Manager

The house manager is the head of the front of house staff and is responsible for everything relating to the theater patrons. For performances, stage management works in conjunction with the house manager to coordinate when to open and close the house, and to gather a house count (total number of people in the audience for a given performance; this is often different from the number of ticket sales) and any important information about the audience (injuries, latecomers, dogs, oxygen tanks, etc.). Be sure to include the house manager in all time calls (either over headset or in person) so they have an idea of the progress backstage. Conversely, be sure to also coordinate your time calls with the status of the house. In some places house management will have the final say as to when the show begins.

> Before calling places for actors at the start of the show and after intermission, always make sure to check in with the house manager to see if you need to hold the house for any reason (often latecomers or large crowds).

Opening the House

Opening the house refers to the time prior to a performance when the theater doors are opened to allow the patrons to make their way to their seats. The house typically opens thirty minutes prior to the performance. Before house opens, the preset checklist should be complete, as well as all fight calls, dance calls, mic check, and lights/sound checks. Be sure to check with everyone (house manager, actors, deck crew, and board operators) before allowing the house to open to make sure that everything is ready to go. Unless it is part of the performance, the audience should not see any of the prep work, as this disrupts the illusion of the show. Once the house opens, no one should walk onstage or through the house except front of house personnel.

If absolutely necessary (e.g., a technical problem that needs addressing), it is okay to hold opening the house. Be sure to communicate this information to any front of house personnel. If possible, it is preferable for the work to be done upstage of the main curtain (if one is in use).

Performance Reports

For every performance, the stage manager sends out a performance report to the same people as the rehearsal reports. This report should document the performance and contain any missed cues, any major actor mistakes, injuries, set, prop, and costume repairs, a house count, and the audience response. Like rehearsal reports, send this out by the following morning before the start of the workday, although preferably immediately following the performance (see Appendix R).

Always mention anything that has happened in the performance report; note if it has already been fixed or needs to be. Be as specific as possible, especially about the location of the item in question. "The USR Light" isn't all that helpful if there are eighty USR lights, and "The bedroom unit needs touch-ups" isn't always specific enough.

During performances, keep the promptbook in the theater at the stage manager's station. If something unfortunate were to happen, this insures the show can go on and another person can step in to call the show.

Standby

Stage management is a field that takes time and experience to really learn, but the information contained in this book should lay the groundwork for the basic building blocks of a successful stage manager. A lot of becoming a good stage manager is learning to work collaboratively with many different personality types. Learning to communicate clearly and concisely will save you many headaches down the road.

As made clear by the previous chapters, much of stage management as a job is endless logistics, flawless organization, and stellar communication. However, all of these things can be learned, practiced, improved upon, and perfected with each new show. Even the personality traits discussed in the first chapter exist on a sliding scale. Some directors work best when allowed to do some of their own organizing, while others will need you to micromanage their whole lives in order to keep their heads on straight. Some actors need a firm, commanding hand with clear rules and tangible consequences. Other actors may need a little coddling and an open ear to listen to their frustrations. Some designers need strict deadlines and many little reminders, while others will shrink away from constant nagging and be less efficient as a consequence. Your particular traits will mesh perfectly with certain teams while another stage manager may be a better fit for others. These are not what define a great stage manager.

What separates a decent stage manager from a truly great one on any production is drive and joy. Each new production should be a thrilling prospect—a chance to practice and improve your skills, pick up new ones, and to tackle new, unexpected challenges. If you cannot love your work, stage management is a job you will quickly come to resent and none of the stress will be worth the reward. It will be difficult at times—scheduling may seem unmanageable, an actor may never seem to learn their lines, and each hurdle you overcome may lead to three more you didn't see coming. But the joy of looking back, seeing all that the production was able to overcome, and being such a critical part of a team that puts together something beautiful and meaningful makes the whole process worthwhile.

The back of this book contains a lot of additional information that will help you grow as a stage manager. We highly suggest you take the time to look through the appendices and additional resources in detail. Use the examples as a jumping-off point for your own forms and templates. Read the suggested books to grow and expand your knowledge base to make you a better stage manager and theatrical artist/collaborator. Remember that you can always grow and learn new things; never stop learning, never stagnate or stop evolving the way you do things, and most importantly, never stop enjoying the work that you do—take pride in it and have fun.

GO!

Glossary

Actor's Equity Association (AEA) A union for theatrical actors and stage managers. Commonly referred to as Equity, AEA, or Union. Theaters or productions working with AEA actors must follow all union rules so stage managers should acquaint themselves with the policies and guidelines before working on any AEA productions. Information packets and all necessary paperwork are available on their website: www.actorsequity.org/

Apron The area of the stage floor downstage of the plaster line. Commonly this extends over the pit and is often curved.

Architect's Scale Ruler This tool is used to measure drawings that have been drawn to a certain scale in order to translate it into full-scale measurements. The stage manager will primarily use this for taping out the set for rehearsals.

Arena A theater in which the audience surrounds the entire stage. There is no "upstage" and "downstage" but rather the action takes place in 360 degrees to cater to the whole audience. Also commonly referred to as "Theater in the round."

Batten Long, typically cylindrical pipes hung above the stage, used to hang scenery, curtains, and lighting instruments. These can be dead hung (permanently hung at a specific height) or rigged on a pulley system, meaning they can be brought in and out via the flyrail or automation computer if the theater uses electric winches.

Blackbox A typically square or rectangular room usually painted completely black, created to be a "flexible" space, designed to be set in any of the different types of stage configurations.

Blocking/Staging The movement or path of the actors throughout the production. This term is used both as a definition of the type of rehearsal in which the director and the actors discover the movement of the production (a blocking or staging rehearsal) and as a definition of the movement itself (blocking notes or the blocking).

Board The slang or shortened term for the light and sound control consoles or "boards." The "board ops" operate these under the direction of the stage manager.

Booth This is the room or place in the theatre where the lightboard / soundboard are located. Typically this is found at the back of the house, often above the audience.

Brush-up Rehearsal/Pick-up Rehearsal A rehearsal that is scheduled in-between longer breaks in performances. At times these may also be scheduled if a performances has gone especially badly and the stage manager feels that the actors/crew may need a "brush-up" on what they are supposed to be doing. This type of rehearsal may also be scheduled if a last-minute change in crew or casting occurs (injury, sickness, family emergency)

CAD Computer-Aided Design. Programs such as Vectorworks and AutoCAD are commonly used by set designers and lighting designers to draft their designs electronically.

Callboard The callboard is where the company goes for important information regarding the production. It is often a corkboard or similar bulletin board and is placed in a centralized location easily accessible in the theater. It typically includes a daily sign-in sheet, the rehearsal calendar, the daily/weekly rehearsal schedule, fittings schedules, and important notifications or announcements. Online callboards are steadily increasing in use, although usually in addition to a physical callboard.

Calls Refers to a specific time or chunk of time when an actor, crew, or other production team member is expected to arrive and be present at a rehearsal or performance.

Caster Wheels used to allow for the movement of scenic pieces on and offstage. Casters can either be swivel ("Smart") meaning they are free to swivel in any director or straight ("dumb") meaning they can only roll along a fixed line depending on the direction in which they are mounted.

Catches When a crew member or actor stands ready backstage to grab a prop or costume piece from an actor with a quick transition who doesn't have time to return it themselves.

Catwalk (Cats) The area above the audience that provides additional lighting positions. Depending on the theater, spotlights may also be located and run from the catwalks.

Center Line The imaginary line that runs vertically upstage to downstage along the center of the stage, splitting the stage into equal halves. Commonly used by stage managers as the y-coordinate in conjunction with plaster line to help with accuracy in tape-out, as well as for marking dance numbers and quarters.

Character Breakdown Character breakdowns provide basic information regarding the characters in the show: name, relationship to other characters in the play, age, brief description. Typically distributed or provided during the audition process.

Cold Reading When an actor is asked to present a piece of text that they have not prepared before the audition. They may be given a few minutes to review or may be asked to read it on the spot. This is especially common during callbacks.

Company Manager Responsible for managing the company (actors, designers, and technicians), including any travel, accommodation, and other day-to-day needs as required

Concept Meeting Meetings for which the focus is to discuss the artistic vision of the production. This is the time during which the director presents their concept and the designers throw around their ideas for their various design elements to help achieve that concept. These tend to be more brainstorming sessions rather than a time for final decisions and logistics.

Costume Shop The space in which costumes are created and/or altered. This can either be located in the theater or off-site.

Crossover Paths that actors can take backstage to get from stage right to stage left without being seen by the audience. This can be a hallway just outside of the theater, a space behind a curtain upstage, or even outside around a building.

Cue Light A light mounted offstage that serves as a visual cue. It is controlled by the stage manager at their station and can be used to cue anyone from stage crew to actors to fly crew to the conductor. These are especially common when a vocal cue is not possible (lack of headsets or backstage communication) or on productions with a large number of simultaneous or quick sequence cues. The light is turned on to indicate a standby. When the light is switched off, this indicates a GO for the cue.

Cue to Cue (Q2Q) A technical rehearsal in which the show is run through in order, skipping, just as the name suggests, from cue to cue. Used to help acquaint the stage manager, tech crew, and actors with the cues of the show.

Cueing The time when the lighting designer sets the level (intensity) of each and every light for the show. This is typically done during "dark time" when all the work lights on the stage can be turned off and no one is working onstage. These levels are usually programmed into a computerized lighting console for recall later during the process and show. *In a perfect world this happens and is completed before the tech process because tech is for all technical areas, not just lighting.

Cyclorama (Cyc) A (typically) white curtain stretched tightly and cleanly along the back edge of the stage and used for lighting and/or projection. Light gray and blue are also common colors.

Dance Numbers A visual breakup of the stage floor used in musicals and other shows with dance or choreography. The breakup is indicated by numbers taped or written at consistant increments along the downstage edge of the stage, starting at 0 at center stage and growing larger as they move offstage in both directions.

Deck Another term for the stage. Used commonly in reference to the stage crew (aka deck crew).

Dramaturge Provides information about the script, time period, writer, and anything else relevant to the production. They may provide a glossary if there are a lot of unusual words or find articles that give context to an aspect of the setting of the play.

Dress Rehearsal (Dress) A rehearsal that takes place after tech, in which all elements of the production are put together, including all technical elements. These rehearsals are meant to simulate a performance but without the audience and should be run without stopping unless absolutely necessary.

Dry Tech A technical rehearsal in which everyone except the cast sits in the performance space and goes through the show cue by cue and (if necessary) scene shift by scene shift. This gives the director a chance to look at and listen to each cue. It also allows the stage manager to become familiar with the cues and where they will be called.

Electrics Battens that hang above the stage and are designated for hanging lighting instruments. Typically these are numbered from downstage to upstage (Electric 1 being most downstage). In some theaters these are always the same, in others they are flexible and can be moved anywhere.

Elevation A term used in drafting to indicate a front, side, or back view of scenic elements.

Entrance/Exit Flow Chart Very similar to a French scene breakdown, this charts every entrance and exit of every character throughout the show. This can be very useful as reference while scheduling rehearsals and for determining when actors are offstage during the production.

Fight Call A practice run of all choreographed fights in a production. It typically takes place 15–30 minutes (depending on the number of fights) before the rest of the cast is called for rehearsals and performances and is run by the stage manager and the fight captain.

Fire Curtain Only found in larger proscenium theatres, this curtain is made of a flame-retardant material, it lowers typically around the plaster line. The curtain can usually be triggered manually in case of a fire, most fire curtains also have a fusible link (link that melts at a relatively low temperature) and will trigger automatically if the heat reaches a certain point. The fire curtain line (where the curtain will fall) may not be obscured by any permanent scenery or props, anything placed on the line (furniture, hinged flat/wall) must be easily movable in the event of a fire. If something will be placed in the fire curtain line a plan should be made with the crew during technical rehearsals about how to clear the fire line in the event of a fire. Fire curtain regulations vary by local legislation.

Fire Proofing Coating a scenic element, costume, or prop with a fire retardant to reduce its flammability. This is especially important if the item is near open flame (candle, lit match etc).

Flat A piece of scenery that typically makes up a wall. Hollywood flats are hard flats covered with Luaun and Broadway flats are soft flats covered with muslin. Flats can be constructed in all shapes and sizes but typical stock sizes are 2 × 8, 4 × 8, 4 × 10, 4 × 12.

Flyrail Area in the wings where the machinery controlling the fly system is housed and where the fly crew will run the show.

Fly Space The area above the stage used for storing hung scenery and curtains. Not available in all theaters and the amount and height of fly space varies from space to space.

Focus The time when a lighting designer points and positions the lights where they need to be for the show. If an electrics crew exists this will be done by the crew, with the designer indicating proper placement and location.

Foley Sound effects that are created live backstage, rather than with pre-recorded sound effects running through a soundboard.

French Scene Breakdown French Scenes are delineated by any entrance/exit of an actor (there may be multiple french scenes in a single book scene). This type of breakdown is useful for plays that are not broken down into acts and scenes.

Front of House (FOH) This refers to the area of the theater through which the patrons are taken and also to the staff that manage it. This includes the box office, the lobby, the bar or concession area, etc. The personnel includes box office managers, house manager, bar staff, and ushers.

Gaffers Tape Colloquially known as gaff, this is one of the most commonly used tapes in the theatrical world. It is a fabric tape, which allows it to be ripped cleanly and easily on two planes. It comes in a variety of colors and typically doesn't leave residue like duct tape. However, it is a strong adhesive and can easily pull off paint or other surface finishes. Gaff tape, especially cheaper off-brands, can get very sticky in hot weather.

Gel A colored piece of polyester or polycarbonate that is placed in front of theatrical lights to color them.

Ghost Light A single bulb, typically on a stationary or rolling stand, that is left illuminated on the stage of a theater when no one is actively using the space. Practically, it is there for safety purposes so no one trips over the set or off the stage in the dark. The name originates from the theatrical superstition that ghosts inhabit all theaters. It is said that the light is left illuminated to allow the ghosts to perform, thus appeasing them and reducing the likelihood of supernatural mischief.

Glow Tape Glow tape is specialized tape coated with photo-luminescent pigments that absorb and store energy from ambient light. In a blackout, the tape glows, allowing actors to see without needing to wait for their eyes to adjust. Most commonly used for safety purposes, glow tape only works when it has been exposed to ambient light (for example, stage lights), so it is best for use on stage where there is consistent exposure. When used backstage with limited light exposure, the tape must be "charged" in order to glow (a flashlight works well for this). However, white gaffers tape is a better alternative.

Go The magic word in all theatrical performances, during techs, dresses, and performances, it should never be used unless the command to "GO" is actually being given. To avoid confusion over headsets and intercoms spelling the world "G-O" is the best way to avoid prematurely moving forward.

Gobo (Template; Pattern) A lighting accessory used in theatrical lights, commonly made of either cut metal or etched glass, used to project an image or pattern.

God Mic A handheld microphone used by the stage manager and/or director during technical rehearsals and performances to communicate with the entire company without the need for shouting.

Grand Drape (Main Drape, Main Curtain, Main Rag, Act Curtain) The main, most downstage curtain in a proscenium theater.

Green Room A lounge area for the company. Typically located backstage of the theater. This is a common area to house the callboard, to gather the company for announcements, and may sometimes double as an extra dressing room.

Grid The area above the stage used for hanging lighting instruments and sound equipment. Also can be used when referring to the steel structure holding up the overstage rigging mechanics

Groundplan The bird's-eye view of the set, drawn to scale. This will be provided by the scenic designer and will be used for taping out the set for rehearsals and for reference throughout the production process. It can also be scaled down and used in the blocking script.

Hand Prop Props that are handled and moved on/offstage by the actors (e.g., cups, books, pencils).

Handoff When a crew member or actor stands ready backstage with a prop or costume piece to be handed to an actor with a quick transition who doesn't have time to grab it themselves.

Heads A common warning called out when someone working overhead drops something. The proper response is to cover one's head with one's arms and move away from the direction of the "heads" call. Do not look up and watch what is falling.

Headshot Headshots are professional quality photos provided by the actors. They are typically 8" x 10" photos of an actor from mid-chest up, and can be either portrait or landscape and black and white or color depending on personal preference.

House The term used to refer to the audience and/or the area in the theater in which the audience is placed for a performance.

House Lights Used during preshow and postshow to light the audience to help with seating. These are typically dimmer than work lights and help to set the mood for the performance.

Legs Vertical curtains, typically black, used at intervals on the sides of a proscenium to help mask the wings from the audience.

Libretto The combined script and vocal score used for most musicals.

Light Hang The time when all the lights are hung up in the theater in the location specified by the lighting designer. The lights are also typically plugged in and gel (color) may be added at this time, although sometimes the color is added during focus.

Light Plot A graphic representation of the layout of the lighting instruments for a given production. The light plot includes information such as type of instrument, color, channel, dimmer, and other relevant information. This will be provided by the lighting designer or the master electrician.

Line 1) The words spoken by a character in the text of the play.

2) Request from an actor for a prompt when they have forgotten their words.

Line Notes Notes taken by the stage manager once actors are off-book, tracking any errors made in the text, including paraphrasing, skipped words, and inaccurate ordering of words or phrases. Some stage managers will also take note of when an actor calls for line. These notes are split up by actor and distributed on an individual basis after each rehearsal off-book.

Load-In The day (or days) in which the technical elements of the production are brought into the theater. This is when the set is installed, the lights are hung, the sound is set up, and the costumes, props, and furniture are moved into the theater. Typically this takes place a few days to a week before tech rehearsals begin.

Marley Tape Translucent tape named for its original use of taping the seams of Marley Floors used for dance. Most common use for stage managers is to help protect spike marks from wear and from pulling up off the floor. This tape comes in multiple different colors, but for this use clear is the best option.

Master Carpenter The lead carpenter on the set-building team. They work closely with the scenic designer and the technical director to create the set.

Master Electrician The lead electrician, typically responsible for hanging, running cables, and focusing all lighting instruments and associated equipment. They work closely with the lighting designer to achieve their plot. This will typically be the person to contact with any technical difficulties with the lighting equipment throughout the run of the production.

Model (White Model) A fully designed miniature 3D version of the set. A white model is typically one color and simply represents the shapes and functions of the set. A full production model will also include accurate textures and colors of the final set for reference.

Monitor Either an audio or video monitor that projects the action on stage in real time. When onstage, this allows the actors to hear themselves as the audience is hearing them to adjust for volume, pitch, etc. for the best performance. When offstage, audio monitors are often mounted in the dressing rooms, hallways, and/or green room for everyone to follow the show and be ready for their cues. Depending on the calling location, a video and/or audio monitor will be mounted at the stage manager's podium for use in calling cues.

Not To Scale (NTS) This abbreviation is commonly found on drawings and indicates to the observer that this drawing is not in any scale. It has simply been sketched out for quick reference or design concepts. Do be careful not to use NTS drawings for tape out!

Off-book Refers to when actors are expected to have fully memorized their lines so they no longer have their scripts in hand during rehearsal. Also true of musical numbers.

Page To hold a door or curtain open to allow for smoother exits/entrances by actors or crew members.

Paper Tech A meeting involving the stage manager, director, lighting designer, and sound designer at which you talk through the script in order and take notes about cue names, placement, and intent.

Performance Report A report generated to note what happened during a performance. Performance reports should include a brief overview and evaluation of the performance as well as relevant notes for every department, noting late cues, broken items, and absences or injuries if they occur. These are to be distributed to the production and design team following each performance and with enough time to address any repair or maintenance notes before the next performance.

Period Piece A production which takes place during a very specific time period in history. Although it could refer to any time period, this term is commonly used when referring to pieces taking place during the Romantic era and usually indicates the need for elaborate costumes and sometimes wigs.

Personal Prop Props that are kept in an actor's possession throughout the show (e.g. pocket watches, fans, canes).

Photo Call A dedicated call used to take staged production photos, usually for use in portfolios and archives, rather than publicity. Commonly takes place during dress rehearsals or sometime during the run of the performances and typically lasts around one hour. This call should be arranged and run by the stage manager.

Pit 1) The orchestra

2) The area in the theater designated for the orchestra. In proscenium theaters, this is commonly located below the apron, underneath the stage, with the conductor positioned facing upstage so as to see both the orchestra and the actors.

Plaster Line In proscenium theaters, this is an imaginary horizontal line that runs the width of the stage at the proscenium arch (mimics the line of the grand curtain, whether one is present or not). In non-prosceniums, this line can be arbitrarily designated. Commonly used by stage managers as the x-coordinate in conjunction with the center line to help with accuracy in tape-out.

Platform A piece of scenery that is walked on and can be used to create an additional level onstage. When casters are added it becomes a wagon (see wagon). Typically a 2-inch by 4-inch frame with a plywood top.

Play The text of the show (i.e. script).

Practical An audio or lighting element of the set that functions—a bedside lamp that lights up, a cell phone that rings, a radio that plays from its own speaker, an LED "Open" sign on a shop door, etc. This may be controlled by the actors onstage or hooked up to the light/sound board and controlled by a cue.

Preshow The time prior to the start of a performance. This is the time during which all actors and crew members prepare for the show, including setting props and scenic elements, getting into costume, hair, and makeup, and checking lighting and sound systems to make sure everything is running smoothly.

Prep Week The week preceding the start of rehearsals during which a stage manager prepares for the productions (including paperwork, rehearsal space prep, creating the promptbook, and any communication with the company in preparation for rehearsals).

Preview Essentially a trial performance for an audience. These performances take place prior to opening night, allowing the cast to perform for an audience and the creative team to continue to make adjustments to the show to make the best performance possible. Typically tickets are sold for a discount and the audience is warned that it is possible the show might be stopped mid-performance for adjustment or technical difficulty, although this rarely occurs.

Producer Manages the overall financial functions of a theatrical organization. They hire and fire, sign paychecks, and typically have final say over all decisions.

Production A specific company's interpretation of a script (a fully realized performance of a particular text). The performance as a whole, including all technical elements.

Production Analysis A detailed breakdown of the text, created by the stage manager during prep week, that accounts for all design elements mentioned in the script. Used as a baseline for the final design decisions for a particular production.

Production Meeting Meetings for which the focus is to discuss the logistics and progress of the production. Typically take place once a week during the rehearsal period with the whole creative team in attendance. This is the time to check in on progress of plots, set and costume building, the prop search, budgets, and to answer/clarify any questions that have arisen during rehearsals.

Promptbook The promptbook, sometimes called the "Show Bible" or "The Book," is a binder containing any and all important information pertaining to the show as well as the script. This book is created and maintained by the stage manager.

Prop (Property) Anything movable or portable on a set. Any item that cannot be classified as scenery, electrics, or wardrobe falls under this category. Furniture is considered a prop in most theatres, although there are some exceptions.

Props Designer An individual tasked with designing the props for a production. Typically, props designers are only found on shows wherein many of the props must be built by hand (for example, shows involving puppetry). In some companies, the props designer may double as the props master or these might be two separate people.

Props Master The person responsible for gathering and shopping for props. Depending on the theatre and staff this may be done in concert with a props designer or the scenic designer.

Proscenium The most common type of theatrical stage. It is easily identifiable by the iconic proscenium arch that frames the opening of the stage and the audience seated on only one side of the stage. These theaters typically have a large amount of wing space and fly space, which allow for large productions with elaborate sets.

Quarters Another type of visual breakup for a stage, similar to Dance Numbers, used to help dancers place themselves accurately for choreography. For this, the stage is broken up into equal quarter sections, with center stage marked and then halfway offstage on either side. Some choreographers may request 1/8th marks as well for more accuracy.

Quick Change A costume change that must take place in a constricted amount of time. These commonly take place in the wings or behind the set, rather than in the dressing rooms, and often require an extra person or two to assist.

Raked Stage A stage built on an incline, with the area of the stage closest to the audience the lowest and gradually rising as it moves to the back of the stage. These were common long ago when the audience were all seated or standing on the same level, so the raked stage allowed for more people to see the action. The origin of the terms "upstage" and "downstage" come from these types of stages, when downstage was literally down and upstage was up. Raked stages are a safety hazard and so are no longer commonly found.

Rehearsal Prop A stand-in prop of similar size, shape, and weight to the final prop that is used during rehearsals. The stage manager is often in charge of finding and keeping track of the rehearsal props.

Rehearsal Report A report generated to note what happened during rehearsal as well as any questions or changes there may be. It should be comprehensive in the information it includes and be distributed to the production and design teams immediately following every rehearsal.

Rendering A digital or physical drawing depicting the set as it will appear in 3D.

Run Light (Clip Light) Colored light bulbs or dark-gelled lights (traditionally blue) used to help ease navigation backstage in the dark during performances.

Run Sheet Indicates scenic shifts and costume changes (usually only quick changes or complicated ones that are relevant to the run crew). This also tracks prop movement throughout the show.

Run-Through A rehearsal in which large sections or the full show are run with minimal or no stops. The intent is to build continuity and allow the cast and director to get a feel for the show as a whole.

Scale A term used in drafting to indicate the size of a drawing or model in relation to the real size. Common scales are 1/4" and 1/2" in US Standard, 1:5, 1:10, and 1:20 in Metric.

Scale Ruler Typically a triangular ruler that on each side and end contain a different scale, used for measuring draftings printed in scale.

Scene Shop The space in which the set is built. This can either be located in the theater or off-site.

Scenic Breakdown A piece of paperwork created by the stage manager that gives a quick reference of each scene in a script. It details such information as Act/scene, page numbers, characters in the scene, location of the scene, and a brief description of the action for easy identification.

Scenic Charge Individual that works closely with the scenic designer and is in charge of painting the set.

Score The sheet music for a musical. This is usually located at the end or in a separate book than the script. The conductor's score is the most complete and will include all music in the production. Many rented scripts will provide chorus-vocal books per character that include only the musical numbers that that character sings.

Set 1) The scenic elements that create the physical world in which the production takes place. It may be one single unit that stays the same throughout the production or be made up of many different pieces that move, change, and transform throughout the show.

2) A term meaning to place an item or items on stage in a predetermined location.

Set Dressing Prop items that are used for the purpose of decorating the set and lending to the design, rather than for practical use by the actors (e.g., mirrors, vases, lamps, picture frames, window dressing, rugs).

Sides Selected scenes or portions of scenes from a play to be used as audition material. Usually these only involve a few characters and are only a few pages long.

Sightlines What the entire audience can see unobstructed from their seat in the house.

Sing-through Similar to a table read, this is a chance for the cast to sing through all of the songs in a musical production. This takes place in the first week of rehearsals and is typically run by the music director.

Sitzprobe A musical rehearsal that takes place prior to tech in which the orchestra and the actors perform together for the first time. This is a chance to set tempos, volume, and other musical adjustments as necessary. If microphones are used during the production, these are set up and run by the sound board operator to set levels. This rehearsal should be co-run by the stage manager and the musical director, with input from the director.

Soundscape Sound design that creates the audio world of the show. Different than sound cues (such as a gunshot, doorbell, phone ring, etc.), this is the ambient sound of the outside world (the background sound of battle, gunshots, men shouting, and shells in a war; birds chirping, dogs barking, children playing and wind blowing at a park, crickets chirping at night) and helps to give body and realism to a show.

Spacing Rehearsal Typically the first rehearsal in the theater in which the director and choreographer take the time to take the blocking and spacing created in the rehearsal space and translate it to the actual stage, especially as it relates to the scenery. Blocking may be changed and spike marks may move in order to best fit the space, sightlines, and the needs of the production.

Spike A semi-permanent indication of where a prop, set piece, or person is meant to be set onstage, marked to ensure consistency from performance to performance. These are most commonly marked using spike tape, a type of gaff tape that comes in a large variety of colors for easy identification.

Spike Tape A type of gaff tape, usually cut to 1/2 inch width, that is used for taping out sets and for spiking furniture, props, and set pieces for consistent placement throughout the run of the production. It comes in a large variety of colors, including neon and glow, to allow for color coding and easy identification.

Stage Directions In reference to within the text of a play, stage directions are the notes included regarding action, sound or lighting effects, and other details regarding the visual aspects of the production not portrayed in the lines. Typically given in italics.

In reference to the physical stage, stage directions are the guidelines that dictate which area of the stage someone or something is (Upstage, Downstage, Stage Right, Stage Left, and Center).

Stage Manager's Kit A toolbox (sometimes literally) of basic supplies that might be necessary in rehearsal or in performance. Depending on the theatre, a stage manager may use a personal kit or the theatre may have one for use by the stage manager.

Stage Manager's Station The area in the theater where a stage manager is stationed during the performance to call their cues. Depending on the theater and the production, this may be in the booth or backstage in the wings. Commonly this is a podium with space for the promptbook and has a headset, a monitor, and cue light control. Sometimes known as the calling station.

Standby A warning call given over headset to crew members to indicate an upcoming cue. Standbys are given about half a page prior to a cue being called. Depending on the production, number of cues being given, and personal preference of the stage manager, crew members may reply to this with "Standing by", "Heard", by repeating the cue name, or any other preferred response to indicate that they have heard the cue and are ready to take it when given the "GO."

Start and Stop A type of technical rehearsal similar to a cue-to-cue in that it is meant to acquaint everyone with the technical elements of the show, and allow the stage manager time to learn the correct placement of all the cues. These are typical on shows that are heavily cued, like musicals, so rather than skipping from cue to cue, this type of rehearsal runs through the majority of the show; starting, stopping, resetting, and rerunning as necessary until everyone understands what needs to happen.

Strike 1) The time following the closing performance during which all elements of the production are taken down and the theater space is cleaned out and reset for the next production. Commonly takes place immediately following the final performance or in the day or two afterwards.

   2) A term meaning to take offstage.

Stumble-Through A rehearsal in which large sections or the full show are run with the intent of not stopping. This is the first time that section or sections will have been run as a full unit and tend to be clunky and have mistakes, hence the name "stumble."

Table Read The very first rehearsal for a play in which the whole cast sits around a table and reads through the entire script, each reading his or her role. The stage manager may be asked to read the stage directions aloud or provide sound effects. Also known as a read-through.

Table Work Rehearsals in which the goal is to work slowly through the script, stopping to talk about character, pacing, story background, tone, etc. These most commonly take place during the first week of rehearsal and ideally include the full cast.

Tabs Curtains that mask the wings from view of the audience.

Tape Out The groundplan for a set represented in full scale by tape on a rehearsal or stage floor for use in rehearsal until the set is available. This should be completed by the stage manager prior to the first blocking rehearsal and should include all major elements of the set.

Technical Rehearsal (Tech) Rehearsals that take place after load-in and are used to integrate all technical elements of the production, with the exception of costumes. These are usually long, full-day rehearsals and can be frustrating, hectic, and difficult. These rehearsals, as well as dress rehearsals and previews, typically take place in the week up to opening which is commonly referred to as Tech Week (or, colloquially, Hell Week, as there are usually high emotions and minimal sleep).

Text The script (see Play).

Thrust A thrust stage typically has audience on three sides of the stage. Thrust theaters typically have smaller scenic elements because the audience needs to be able to see across the stage and large elements will obstruct the view of the audience on the sides.

Tracking The term used for monitoring of where props, set pieces, costumes, and sometimes actors travel throughout the run of a show. This is very important in terms of making sure that everything is where it needs to be at any given time so that no actor is ever left without the prop they need. Sometimes tracking of a single prop is impossible due to traffic patterns and availability of actors/crew, so multiple of the same prop will need to be acquired.

Turntable A round piece of scenery that rotates and can contain multiple scenes or scenic pieces depending on its size.

Understudy A cast member that is responsible for learning the lines, blocking, and choreography of an assigned character in case of injury, emergency etc.

Union 1) IATSE, is the International Alliance of Theatrical Stage Employees. In larger cities many theatres employ IATSE members as Stage Hands, while some theatres are considered "Union Houses" and only hire union members.

    2) USA-829 is part of IATSE, but is specifically for designers.

    3) See Actors' Equity Association above.

Ushers Members of the house staff that help people find their seats, answer questions, and give directions around the theatre.

Visual Cue A cue that an operator takes on their own rather than from a verbal cue from stage management to ensure perfect timing.

Vomitorium (Vom) An aisle that runs through the audience that acts as an entrance/exit for the actors during a show. These are most commonly found in thrust and arena theaters.

Wandelprobe A rehearsal where actors, the orchestra and blocking come together for the first time. Essentially, a sitzprobe with movement and possibly props.

Wagon A rolling platform mounted on castors that typically houses a set piece.

Wings The offstage right and left sides of the stage, unseen by the audience. The wings are typically blocked from view by a combination of walls and curtains and used to store props, set pieces, and actors waiting for their entrances.

Work Lights (Works) Overhead lights in a theater or other performance space. Usually fluorescents or other similar source. Most typically they will light both the audience and the stage areas and are used during working hours (not during the performance).

American to English Glossary

American	English
Bells, Chimes	Barbells (chimes that play in the lobby five minutes before show comes down to alert front of house staff)
Blackout curtain, full stage black	Full Black
Board, Console	Desk
Booth	Box
Building the set onstage	Fit Up
Call the half-hour at 30 minutes to curtain	Call the half-hour at 35 mins to curtain
Calls include Half, Fifteen, Five, Places	Calls include Half, Quarter, Five, Beginners
Consumables, Perishables	Comestibles
Cueing	Plotting
Curtain Warmers	Tab warmers (lights on the house curtain before it rises)
Flashlight	Torch
Gaff	Gaffa
Headsets, radios, walkie-talkies	Comms, Cans
House closed	Clearance (front of house gives to stage manager when lobby clear and ready to start show)
House Curtain	Tabs
Intermission	Interval
Load-In	Load-In (or simply In)
Masking Softgoods	Blacks
Monitors in dressing rooms	Show Relay
Monitors in dressing rooms, God mic	Tannoy (speaker system in dressing rooms used by stage manager to communicate backstage)
Opening Night	First Night
Paper Tech	Cue Synopsis
Performance Report	Show Report
Places	Beginners
Plaster Line	Setting Line
Preshow Checklist	Checks
Production Calendar	Provisional Schedule

Promptbook	Book, Prompt Copy
Props Checklist	Tick Check
Raised platform of any shape or size	Rostra
Reset	Reset (at end of show before next)
Reset (props, set, costumes, lighting, etc.)	Setting Back
Run Sheets	Running Plot
Scrim	Gauze
Special Thanks	Credits
Spikes	Marks
Stage Left / Right	Prompt Side / Off Prompt (P and OP, usually P is SR but this can vary)
Stage Manager's Podium (Down Stage Left)	Corner, Prompt Corner
Stage Right	Opposite Prompt
Strike	Get Out
Tapeout	Mark Out / Mark Up
Tech (Tech rehearsal)	Technical
Tech Week	Pre-Production Week
To forget a line	To dry
Theatrical Housing	Digs
Traveler	Split Curtain
Turntable	Revolve
Wagon	Truck

Appendices

Appendix A
Production Analysis

Act.Sc.Pg	Time/Place	Entrance/Exit/Costume	Sets	Props	Lights	Sound
1.1.3	Manhattan Apartment	En: Sylvia, Greg		Leash, newspaper		*Romantic music intro (something suggesting NYC)
1.1.4		On Stg: Sylvia, Greg	Couch, Greg chair	A letter (Dennis), bar stuff		
1.1.8		En: Kate		Large tote (Kate)		
1.1.9			Kate desk			
1.1.14		Ex: Kate				
1.1.15		En: Kate		2 drinks, phone		*Phone ring
1.1.16		Ex: Greg		Books, notebook, pencil (Kate, in tote)		
1.1.21		En: Greg				
1.1.24				*Puddle? (Have to be real?)		
1.1.27		Ex: Kate En: Kate Ex: Greg, Sylvia		Spray cleaner, cloth		
1.2.28	Park	Ex: Kate En: Greg, Sylvia				*Nature music, bird sounds, dog barks
1.2.29		Ex: Sylvia En: Tom (Jeans, windbreaker, baseball cap)				
1.2.31		En: Sylvia				
1.2.32		Ex: Sylvia				
1.3.35	Apartment (Mid August)	Ex: Tom, Greg En: Kate (watch), Greg (different, informal shirt)		Books, papers (Kate)	(Mid August)	*Domestic music

(Continued)

Continued

No.	Setting	Characters	Props	Pink Light	Sound/Music
1.3.37		Ex: Greg En: Greg, Sylvia (new hairdo, bow, corny outfit)			Lush advertising music
1.3.39		Ex: Kate			
1.3.40		Ex: Sylvia, Greg En: Kate (Bathrobe)	Cell phone	Night	Phone ringing
1.4.41	Late at night, Urban Setting	Ex: Kate En: Greg, Sylvia		Late at night	Urban and moody music
1.5.47	Night, Airport waiting area	Ex: Greg, Sylvia En: Kate (raincoat, watch), Greg	Bag, books, notebooks (Kate)	Night	Airport music, jet sounds, Prerecorded announcement
1.5.49		En: Sylvia			Music modulates to piano accompaniment ("Ev'ry Time We Say Goodbye"), Prerecorded announcement
1.5.50			Plane ticket		
1.6.51	Daytime, Apartment	Ex: Kate, Greg, Sylvia En: Phyllis (Jacket), Kate	Stack of mail	Daytime	"Ev'ry Time" music ends, urban and hectic music at scene change
1.6.52		Ex: Kate (take Jacket off) En: Kate			
1.6.55		Ex: Kate En: Kate	Two drinks		
1.6.58		Ex: Kate En: Kate	Scotch (liquid)		
1.6.60		En: Greg, Sylvia			
1.6.62		Ex: Sylvia	Red ball, dog treats		
1.6.63		Ex: Kate			
1.6.64		Ex: Kate En: Sylvia, Kate	Scotch bottle		

Act.Sc.Pg	Time/Place	Entrance/Exit/Costume	Sets	Props	Lights	Sound
1.6.67		Ex: Phyllis, Sylvia, Kate				
1.6.68		En: Kate, Sylvia Ex: Sylvia				
1.6.72		En: Sylvia		Woman's shoe		
1.6.73		Ex: Greg, Sylvia				
1.6.74		En: Sylvia				
1.6.75						*Offstage sound of Greg banging dish
1.6.77		En: Greg		Dog dish w/kibble	Quick B/O	
				INTERMISSION		
2.1.81	Day (Autumn), The Park	On Stg: Greg, Sylvia	"Park bench"		Warm Autumn light, suggestion of foliage	"Autumn in New York", bird sounds, dogs yapping OS
2.1.82		Ex: Sylvia En: Tom (Watch, Cigarette, lighter/matches)				Louder barking/yapping OS
2.1.86		En: Sylvia				
2.1.87		Ex: Sylvia				
2.1.91		Ex: Tom En: Sylvia				
2.2.95	Apartment	En: Kate, Greg, Sylvia		Document (Kate)		English Renaissance music (Purcell?), Noises OS
2.2.102		Ex: Kate				
2.3.103	Marriage counselor office	Ex: Greg, Sylvia En: Leslie (Unisex outfit), Kate	Chair and desk, Venetian blinds	Notes (notebook?) – Leslie (Extra copies needed, torn each night)		Music (Philip Glass?)
2.3.105		En: Greg (Watch)				Noises OS

(Continued)

Continued

		Location	Characters	Props	Props	Sound/Music
2.3.106			Ex: Kate			
2.3.114			Ex: Greg / En: Kate / Ex: Leslie			
2.4.115		Apartment	Ex: Kate / En: Greg, Sylvia (Little black dress)	Leash		Music "Now is the Hour" Vera Lynn
2.4.120				Bark Bar (cat-shaped Dog treat)		
2.4.124			Ex: Sylvia / En: Kate			Kate speaks OS
2.4.127			En: Sylvia (First outfit)			
2.4.128			Ex: Greg, Sylvia / En: Sylvia, Greg	All's Well That Ends Well (ppbk)		
2.4.129			Ex: Greg			Greg speaks OS
2.4.130			Ex: Sylvia, Kate / En: Greg, Kate	Red Ball (in sofa cushion)		Door closes OS, Tuba Mirum section of Dies Irae (Verdi Requiem)
2.4.132				Wallet (Greg), small color picture of a dog	*Large, blown-up picture (on cyc?)	
2.4.133						*"Ev'ry Time We Say Goodbye" (Benny Goodman Quartet)
End Of Show						

Appendix A.1
Example Props List

Act/Sc	Page	Prop	Character	Notes	Reh	Final	Pull	Modify	Build	Buy	Status
		Crossbow	Wednesday	Borrow from Jeff							
		Arrow with strap		A strap to sling over shoulder							
		2 fencing foils		Ask Bart			X				
		Bouquet of yellow flowers with card		Flowers must have tops ripped off every night							
		Engagement ring on chain necklace		Talk to D			X				
		Goose with arrow sticking out		Realistic							
		Tassel		Need 2, 1 as puppet and 1 on line						X	
		2 yellow bird puppets		One must have breakable neck, Sesame Street-like bird					X		
		2 rats		Fuzzy and soft, 1 must be rigged to run across stage						X	Ordered
		New York guide book		Check with AAA						X	
		Rapier		Ask Bart			X				
		Coin collecting can		Like March of Dimes					X		
		Loose coin					X				
		Football					X				
		Fester's toupee		Talk to D							
		Tray w/ 4 goblets		Use metal Macbeth goblets			X				
		2 cigars		1 must look lit							
		Family photo Abby		Leather-bound book			X				Ordered
		Alice's wine glass		Reuse Goblets				X			
		Jeweler's loupe		Talk to D							

Item	Character	Description					Notes
Wagon of vials and bottles		One bottle must be green and identifiable, small red wagon and shelves			X	X	
Banquet table		4 sections, red tablecloth and black runner			X	X	
Table settings for 9		Must be matching, includes napkins	X				
Chalice		Big and pretty, will have a chip of dry ice so it can bubble and foam	X				
Cousin It		Halloween store			X	X	
Grim reaper scythe						X	
Blanket					X	X	
Huge spider	Mr. Beineke	Halloween store			X	X	Ordered Ukulele
Banjolele	Fester		X				
Red apple		Fake plastic	X		X		
Monster puppet		Could be costume?	X				
Telephone		Candlestick Type	X			X	
Valise	Morticia's		X	X		X	
Bull fighter's cape	Gomez	Should match costume	X		X	X	
Rocket backpack		Needs sparking fuse		X			
Lunchbox		Old style with rounded top		X			
Famous airline travel bag			X	X			
Bridal bouquet		Fake dead flowers					
Spyglasses	Ancestor's				X	X	Wait for info from Mac
Black umbrellas (10)		D is handling				X	Costumes
Thing on a pillow with ring		Black satin pillow, trembling finger halloween hand	X		X	X	

(Continued)

Continued

Act/Sc	Page	Prop	Character	Notes	Reh	Final	Pull	Modify	Build	Buy	Status
		Wedding rings	Lucas/Wednesday	Talk to D			X				
		Lightbulb wireless	Fester	Jonathan will figure out							Ordered
		Purple cloth to smash lightbulb									
		Basket of dead rose petals		Spray red petals black (leave holidays)				X			Ordered
		Hand grenade								X	Ordered
		Perambulator		Needs glowing moon baby, black						X	
		Moon cutouts		3' diameter, 1 regular, 1 Donna Reed, 1 James Dean, 1 Hillary Clinton					X		
		Sticker		"I was Mooned at the Addams Family"					X		
		Moon crown		Talk to D							
		Star scepter		Talk to D							
		Working camera		Jonathan will take care of							
		Ancestor personal props		Gambler (gun and holster), Caveman (axe), Jilted Bride (bouquet), Indian (TBD), Puritan (old bible), Doughboy (WW1 rifle w/ sling), Conquistador (sword and scabbard). Talk to D							
		4 poster bed dressing		B/W color scheme							
		Small herb	Grandma	Picked from behind tombstone							

Appendix B
Scenic Breakdown

Director: D. Barnett
Music Director: M. Falk
SM: E. Roth

City of Angels
Scene/Character Breakdown

Act/Sc.	Pages	Location	Musical #s	Characters	Actors
Pro	10	Movie Poster	Prologue	Full Cast	Full Cast
I.1	11–12	Hospital	N/A	Stone, First Orderly, Second Orderly	DJ, Sarah, Meghan
I.2	13–20	Stone's Office, Stine's Office	Double Talk (Alaura/Stone)	Oolie, Stone, Alaura, Stine	Aimee, DJ, Kaisi, Sam
I.3	21–24	Stine's Office, Buddy's Office	Double Talk (Buddy, Stine)	Stine, Buddy, Shoeshine Girl	Sam, Ryan, Annika
I.4	25–26	Stone's Outer Office	N/A	Stone, Oolie	DJ, Aimee
I.5	27–29	Stine's Bedroom	N/A	Stine, Gabby	Sam, Tierre
I.6	30–32	Stine's Bedroom, Stone's Outer Office	What You Don't Know About Women	Gabby, Oolie	Tierre, Aimee
I.7	33–36	Stone's Bungalow	Stay With Me, Look Out for Yourself (Prerecorded), LOFY	Stone, Big Six, Sonny, Jimmy, Angel City Four	DJ, Josh B, Jade, Wes, Elizabeth, Emmy, Keenan, Ehren
I.8	37–40	Buddy's Office	The Buddy System	Buddy, Barber, Donna, Stine	Ryan, Annika, Aimee, Sam
I.9	41–43	Stone's Bungalow	N/A	Stone, Munoz, Pasco	DJ, Josh J, Zhen
I.10	44–45	Blue Note Lounge	With Every Breath	Bobbi, Stone, Munoz, Crowd	Tierre, DJ, Josh J, Sarah, Meghan, Hallie, Alex
I.11	46–47	Blue Note DR	N/A	Stone, Irwin, Bobbi	DJ, Ryan, Tierre
I.12	48–50	Stine's Office, Phonebooth	N/A	Stine, Donna, Man, Oolie	Sam, Aimee, Jade
I.13	51–54	Kingsley Terrace	N/A	Alaura, Peter, Margaret, Stone	Kaisi, Alan, Hallie, DJ
I.14	55–60	Solarium	The Tennis Song	Stone, Alaura, Luther, Mandril, Margaret	DJ, Kaisi, Zhen, Alex, Hallie
I.15	61–63	The Search	Everybody's Gotta Be Somewhere	Stone, Jimmy, Angel City Four, Ensemble	Full Cast **EXCEPT:** Sam, Ryan, Josh J, Aimee, Kaisi, Tierre, Shannon
I.16	64–65	Stone's Bungalow	Lost and Found	Stone, Mallory, Jimmy, Angel City Four	DJ, Shannon, Wes, Elizabeth, Emmy, Keenan, Ehren
I.17	66–67	Donna's Bedroom	N/A	Stine, Donna	Sam, Aimee
I.18	68–70	Stone's Bungalow	N/A	Stone, Mallory, Man	DJ, Shannon, Jade

Scene	Pages	Location	Song		
I.19	71–73	Morgue	N/A	Mahoney, Yamato, Irwin, Stone, Bobbi, Munoz	Alan, Thomas, Ryan (Body), DJ, Tierre, Josh J
I.20	74–78	Buddy's Office	N/A	Buddy, Stine, Anna, Mandril, Woman's Arm, Donna	Ryan, Sam, Annika, Alex, Aimee
I.21	79–86	Morgue, Stine's Office	All You Have to Do is Wait, You're Nothing Without Me	Yamato, Mandril, Munoz, Mahoney, Pasco, Stone, Stine	Thomas, Alex (Body), Josh J, Alan, Zhen, DJ, Sam
II.1	87–88	Recording Studio	Stay With Me (No. 2)	Jimmy, Angel City Four, Hallie	Wes, Elizabeth, Emmy, Keenan, Ehren, Hallie
II.2	89–90	Buddy's Bedroom	N/A	Buddy, Carla	Ryan, Kaisi
II.3	91–92	Jail Cell	N/A	Oolie, Stone, Guard	Aimee, DJ, Zhen
II.4	93	Oolie's Bedroom	You Can Always Count On Me	Oolie	Aimee
II.5	94–97	Donna's Bedroom	You Can Always Count On Me	Donna, Stine	Aimee, Sam
II.6	98–99	Bel-Air Garden	Double Talk (Brunch)	Del, Buddy, Guests, Vargas	Alex, Ryan, Sarah, Annika, Thomas, Meghan, Josh J
II.7	100	Buddy's Library	N/A	Stine	Sam
II.8	101	Jail	N/A	Munoz, Stone	Josh J, DJ
II.9	102–108	Buddy's Library, Shed	N/A	Stine, Avril, Carla, Stone, Big Six, Sonny	Sam, Shannon, Kaisi, DJ, Josh B, Jade
II.10	109–112	Bel-Air Garden	Stay With Me	Jimmy, Angel City Four, Buddy, Carla, Stine, Avril, Del, Guests	Wes, Elizabeth, Emmy, Keenan, Ehren, Ryan, Sam, Shannon, Alex, Thomas, Meghan, Sarah, Annika
II.11	113–114	Alaura's Bedroom	N/A	Stone, Alaura	DJ, Kaisi
II.12	115	Buddy's Office	N/A	Buddy, Avril	Ryan, Shannon
II.13	116–118	Stine's Apartment	It Needs Work	Stine, Gabby	Sam, Tierre
II.14	119–120	Whorehouse Parlor	N/A	Margie, Stone, Bootsie	Meghan, DJ, Sarah
II.15	121–125	Red Room	With Every Breath I Take (Duet)	Bobbi, Stone	Tierre, DJ
II.16	126	Phonebooth	N/A	Oolie	Aimee
II.17	127–132	Solarium	N/A	Alaura, Luther, Stone, Peter, Mallory	Kaisi, Zhen, DJ, Alan, Shannon, Hallie
II.18	133–135	Stine's Office	Funny	Stine, Donna	Sam, Aimee
II.19	136–149	Movie Set	I'm Nothing Without You	Full Cast	Full Cast

Appendix B.1
French Scene Breakdown

Act I, sc. 1 / Act I, sc. 2

Pages	1	2	3	4	5	6	7	8	9	10	11	12	13	14	15	16	17	18	19	20	21	22	23	24	25	26	27	28	29	30	31
Charles		∨										∧												∧	∨	∧∨	∨		∧		∧
Ruth	∨												∨		∨										∨		∨			∨	
Elvira									OS												OS			∧							
Mme Arcati																							∧								
Edith	∨	∧	<∧				<∧		∨∧	∨		∧∨		∧∨																	
Mrs. B		∧					∨					∧														∧					
Dr. B							∨					∧														∧					

Act I, sc. 3

Pages	32	33	34	35	36	37	38	39	40	41	42	43
Charles	∨											∧
Ruth	∨											∧
Elvira								∨				∧
Mme Arcati					∨	∧						
Edith		∧	∨									
Mrs. B												
Dr. B												

Act II, sc. 1 / Act II, sc. 2

Pages	43	44	45	46	47	48	49	50	51	52	53	54	55	56	57	58	59	60	61	62
Charles							∨				∧	∨			∧∨			∧		∧
Ruth		∨					∨			∧	∧			∨	∨		∨			
Elvira					∧∨						∧∨				∧			∧		∧
Mme Arcati								∧												
Edith					∧∨	∨														
Mrs. B												∧	∨		∧					
Dr. B															∧					

Act II, sc. 3 / Act II, sc. 4

Pages	63	64	65	66	67	68	69	70	71	72	73	74	75	76	77	78	79	80	81	82	83	84	85	86
Charles	∨							∧∨				∧	∨										∧∨	∧
Ruth	∨											∧∨	∨							∧	∧			
Elvira			∨									∧										∨		
Edith																		∨					∧	
Mme Arcati	∨		∧					∨				∧	∨											
Mrs. B																								
Dr. B																								

Appendix C
Damage Waiver

A–Z Theatrical Design
1600 First Avenue
Springfield, MO 63701
573.555.8000
www.aztheatricaldesign.com

I _____ understand that Vocal Book #_____ and Promptbook #_____ are being assigned to me and that I may not mark in the books with anything other than light pencil marks. Additionally, I will take good care of the books and return them in the condition they were given to me. If I do not follow the above instructions or otherwise damage or deface the books, I will be responsible for the replacement costs of the rented materials: $55.00 for the vocal book and $75.00 for the promptbook.

_____
Signature and Date

Appendix D
Audition Form

[Show Title]
Audition/Callback Form

PERSONAL INFORMATION

Name _____ Major _____

Home Phone _____ Cell Phone _____ Minor _____

E-mail Address _____ Year _____
What is the best method of contact?

Height _____ Eye Color _____ Hair Color _____
Would you be willing to cut and/or grow out and/or color your hair? □ YES   □ NO

ADDITIONAL INFORMATION

Role(s) auditioning for:_____
If you are not cast in your preferred role, will you accept another part? □ YES   □ NO

If you are not cast in your preferred role, are you interested in backstage crew? □ YES   □ NO

Do you work in a full-time or part-time job?   □ FULL TIME   □ PART TIME   □ NONE
How flexible are your work hours?   □ VERY   □ SOMEWHAT   □ NOT AT ALL

How much notice would you need to change your schedule?

_____

SHOW SPECIFICS

Are you comfortable with being partially nude on stage?   □ YES   □ SOME   □ NO

Are you comfortable with eating a leech onstage?   □ YES   □ SORT OF   □ NO

Do you have any tattoos?   □ YES   □ NO

Do you have any allergies to food? (Please list.)

_____

Any additional special talents? (Please list.)

_____

Rehearsal will typically take place on the following:
Monday, Tuesday, Thursday, Friday—7 p.m.–11 p.m., Saturday—2 p.m.–6 p.m.
Please continue on back.

Please shade in or fill out your weekly schedule including classes, jobs, etc.

	MON	TUES	WED	THURS	FRI	SAT	SUN
8:00 A.M.							
9:00 A.M.							
10:00 A.M.							
11:00 A.M.							
12:00 P.M.							
1:00 P.M.							
2:00 P.M.							

	MON	TUES	WED	THURS	FRI	SAT	SUN
3:00 P.M.							
4:00 P.M.							
5:00 P.M.							
6:00 P.M.							
7:00 P.M.							
8:00 P.M.							
9:00 P.M.							
10:00 P.M.							
11:00 P.M.							

Please list any additional conflicts for August 19th–September 6th below:

Appendix E
Character Descriptions

Agamemnon, King of Mycenae.

The play begins with Agamemnon at a moment of crisis, caught between two contradictory courses of action: he has planned the sacrifice of his daughter, yet seeks to avert it at all costs. Agamemnon is a fully dimensional, complex character, with an irreconcilable dilemma. He has duties toward his family but also toward the Greeks, toward his wife and daughter, and toward his self-serving brother. He is willing to tell lies and to deceive, but he also appears humane and emotionally attached to his daughter. Agamemnon is a character whose downfall is brought about by his inability to assume a firm moral and ethical stance.

Menelaus, King of Sparta, brother to Agamemnon.

Self-centered, vengeful, and unlikable, Menelaus is presented by Euripides as an opponent of Agamemnon. His dramatic function is to attempt to cancel his brother's plan to save Iphigenia, and to shed light on Agamemnon's character through a confrontation that introduces many of the play's themes, most notably the characters' frequent vacillations between opposing points of view. It is only after he has had a change of heart and advocates for the abandonment of the Trojan mission in order to spare Iphigenia's life that Menelaus becomes sympathetic. The important theme introduced by Menelaus when he changes his mind is that of kinship and of the tension between family values and public interests.

Clytemnestra, wife to Agamemnon, mother to Iphigenia.

Not yet the transgressing matricide of Aeschylus' *Oresteia*, Euripides' Clytemnestra is far more of a victim than the revenging victimizer she is destined to become after the Trojan War. In this play, Clytemnestra appears as a devoted wife and loving mother whose hatred and disdain toward her husband emerge in the course of the play as a direct result of Agamemnon's actions. She displays throughout the action a very clear sense of her rights and responsibilities within her marriage and in society at large.

Iphigenia, daughter to Agamemnon and Clytemnestra.

At first a pure, virtuous child, on the verge of womanhood, Iphigenia undergoes perhaps the greatest transformation in the play. She is introduced as a young and impulsive girl, having a childlike affection for her father and showing an innocent disregard for social conventions. When she learns that she and her mother have been deceived by her own father and that she has been brought to Aulis not to wed Achilles, but to be sacrificed to the war effort, she pleads hopelessly and impotently for her life. Yet, by the end of the action, she has grown in maturity and stature into the character who takes the onstage action into her own hands, dictating to everyone else how *they* should deport themselves as she goes off willingly to her own death.

Achilles, famed (and glamorous) hero of Homer's *Iliad*, at this point in time is only "destined" to become one of the most prominent warriors of the Trojan War.

An upper-class young man of late fifth-century Athens, proud of his ancestry and sophistic training, impatient and easily offended, with a strong sense of honor and what is right. But Achilles, for all his self-aggrandizement and pride, is also exposed as inexperienced, immature, self-centered, and even bombastic. He is certainly pragmatic, and he adjusts to the demands of his situation; yet he is a man of principle, too, who is willing to rescue Iphigenia even when his own life is in jeopardy. The character that emblematically stands as a symbol of heroism in the *Iliad*, the single most authoritative poem of the Greek world, is reduced by Euripides to a figure unable to defend Iphigenia and his own heroic identity. His admiration of Iphigenia is an admiration of a heroism he is unable to claim for himself. With its portrayal of Achilles, this play challenges a whole set of values and beliefs that are traditionally associated with his Homeric heroism.

The Old Servant, gifted to Clytemnestra as part of her wedding dowry, and currently in service to Agamemnon at Aulis.

This important "minor" character helps to move the plot forward and also to guide the emotions and reactions of the spectators in a way similar to and as complex as that of the chorus. The old servant triggers Agamemnon's expository speech in the prologue, raises expectations about Achilles' temper, and draws the spectators' attention to Agamemnon's inability to predict, let alone to try to avert, the consequences of his fictitious ruse of a marriage between Achilles and Iphigenia. More importantly, it is the servant who reveals to Clytemnestra and Achilles the prophecy of the sacrifice and the fictitiousness of the wedding, thus setting in motion the second half of the play. Despite its centrality to the tragic plot, the role of the old servant is not without its comic side, and a number of his actions point toward a character whose social status, age, and manners set him distinctly apart from the other characters.

The Chorus of young married women from Chalcis [pronounced "kal-kis"], the town across the strait from the camp of the Greek army at Aulis.

This group of what are essentially "sightseers" has traveled across a body of water to "watch" the famous Greek fleet, about which they apparently have heard a great deal. Euripides' seemingly arbitrary introduction of this group of young women into the play after the expository scene allows the thereafter ever-present Chorus to comment on the action and to intervene in the dialogue segments of the play as detached onlookers. In their "odes," they introduce and reflect on a number of themes that permeate the plot: love and desire, war and peace, as well as marriage and sacrifice. They also offer emotional, moral and mythological filters through which to view what happens on stage. The women of Chalcis, though, are far from impartial and disinterested spectators. Their point of view is subjective and, like the old servant, they collectively create an emotional and psychological lens through which the audience is invited to judge the action.

Appendix F
Weekly Rehearsal Schedule

Monday 1/2

	10–1	Full Co.—meet/greet/read-thru, begin music
	1–2	Lunch/Production Meeting
	2–4	Music
	4–5	Begin *We Go Together* Dance
	5–6	Music
	6–7:30	Dinner break
	7:30–8:30	Block I-1; pages 7–8 (*Alma Mater/Parody*)
	8:30–9:30	Begin blocking I-2; pages 8–16 (*Summer Nights*)

Tuesday 1/3

	10–11:30	Continue blocking I-2; pages 8–16 (*Summer Nights*)
	11:30–1:30	Music
	1:30–2:30	Lunch
	2:30–4	Block I-3; pages 16–18 (*Magic Changes*)
	4–6	Block I-4; pages 18–23 (*Freddy My Love*)
	7–9:30	TBA Music

Wednesday 1/4

	10–12	Block I-5; pages 23–26 (*Greased Lightnin'*)
	12–1	Block I-6; pages 26–28 (*Rydell Fight Song*)
	1–2	Lunch
	2–6	Block I-7; pages 28–34 (*Mooning; Sandra Dee; We Go Together*)
	6–7:30	Dinner break
	7:30–9:30	Stumble-thru Act I

Thursday 1/5

	10–12	*Hand Jive* Dance (Sandy, Johnny Casino, Miss Lynch, Vince Fontaine not needed)
	12–1	Music
	1–2	Lunch
	2–3	Music
	3–6	Block II-1; pages 35–43 (*Shakin' at the High School Hop; Raining on Prom Night; Hand Jive*)
	7–9:30	TBA Music

Friday 1/6

10–11	Block II-3; pages 48–50 (*Alone at a Drive-in Movie*)
11–1	Block II-2; pages 43–48 (*Beauty School Dropout*)
1–2	Lunch
2–3:30	Block II-4; pages 51–55 (*Rock 'n Roll Party Queen; There are Worse Things I Could Do; Sandra Dee Reprise*)
3:30–6	Block II-5; pages 55–59 (*All Choked Up; We Go Together Reprise*)
6–7:30	Dinner break
7:30–9:30	Stumble-thru Act I

Saturday 1/7

A.M.	Run-thru with notes
P.M.	Run-thru with notes

Appendix F.1
Rehearsal Schedule

MAYBE TOMORROW
Rehearsal Schedule—V3

SUNDAY	MONDAY	TUESDAY	WEDNESDAY	THURSDAY	FRIDAY	SATURDAY
26 Rehearsal 1–5 p.m. (A)	**27**	**28** Rehearsal 4–6 p.m. (Jenny Only) (C)	**29**	**30** Rehearsal 4–6 p.m. (Jenny Only) (C)	**31**	**1 AUGUST** Rehearsal 2–7 p.m. (A)
2 AUGUST Rehearsal 1–6 p.m. (A)	**3** Rehearsal 6–9:30 p.m. (A)	**4** Rehearsal 6–10 p.m. (A)	**5** Rehearsal 6–10 p.m. (A)	**6** 2 p.m. Venue Prep (Tomer & Emily Only) Rehearsal 6–10 p.m. (A)	**7** 7 p.m. Costume Pub Crawl (optional)	**8**
9 Toilet-A-Thon Union Square	**10** Rehearsal 6–10 p.m. (A)	**11** Rehearsal 6–10 p.m. (A)	**12** Rehearsal 6–10 p.m. (A)	**13** Rehearsal 6–10 p.m. (A) 10 p.m. Fringe Opening Night Party (E)	**14** Tech 4–6:40 p.m. (F)	**15** 2:45 p.m. Opening! (F) 4:15 p.m. FringePlus Party!
16 5:30–7 p.m. Fringe Teaser	**17** 9 p.m. Performance (F)	**18**	**19**	**20**	**21** 7:45 p.m. Performance (F)	**22**
23 1:15 p.m. Performance (F) 10 p.m. Mid-Festival Relief Party (E)	**24**	**25**	**26**	**27**	**28**	**29** 1:15 p.m. Performance (F)
30 10 p.m. Closing Night Party/Awards Ceremony (E)	**31**	**1 SEPTEMBER**	**2**	**3**	**4**	**5**

Rehearsal Spaces:

A = Goddard Community Center (92nd & Columbus)   B = UWS Apartment (200 Riverside Blvd)   C = The Pit (123 E 24th St.)   E (Fringe Events) = DROM: 85 Ave A (between 5th and 6th Street)   F = Under St. Marks (94 Saint Marks Pl.)

Appendix G
Production Meeting Agenda

On the Town
Southeast MO State University
Production Meeting Agenda
Wednesday, December 2nd, 2015 ~ 11:30 a.m.

General

- Program information. What is the deadline for needing crew information?
- First day of rehearsal after break is January 10th, What information needs to be provided for early house return for cast and shop assistants?
- Check contact sheet for accuracy. Am I missing anyone?
- Bedell move-in date. T&D gets the theatre on February 7th. Crew watch is Feb 18th.
- Next production meeting January 13th, 11 a.m.
- Other business, questions, comments, concerns?

Costumes

- What do we need at the moment from Jim?
- Renderings are in the Dropbox for those who have not seen them yet.
- Fittings needed?
- Number of wardrobe crew needed? Hair and makeup?
- Mic belts. Do we have enough? (X-ref sound)
- When do Jim and his stitcher arrive? Is everything arranged for their arrival?
- Other business, questions, comments, concerns?

Lighting

- Chase light sample lamp
- Moon box from stock? Just under 4'-0"
- Overhire master electrician?
- Other business, questions, comments, concerns?

Sound

- Pit location?
- Number of mics needed?
- Mic belts. Do we have enough? (X-ref costumes)
- Other business, questions, comments, concerns?

Music

- Status of music rehearsal?
- Needs for the pit?
- Other business, questions, comments, concerns?

Props

- Preliminary props list?
- Possible props master?
- Other business, questions, comments, concerns?

Scenic

- Status of scale, PDF, scene-by-scene groundplans?
- Status of drawings?
- Color choices and painters' elevations?
- Overhire?
- Other business, questions, comments, concerns?

Production Meeting Notes

The Heiress
Production Meeting Notes
Monday, July 1st ~ 10:30 p.m.

Scenic:

- Catherine will be sitting in the window seat with a hurricane in Act II, scene 2. We need to make sure that the curtains will not catch on fire (either flame-retardant material or placement onstage).
- The mayor will be lending us the chair set for the Sloper chairs!
- The window seat will be 24 inches tall. There needs to be a discussion between Jonathan and Evie about details on how this will look.
- The baseboards will be made out of 2-inch foam stripping and painted.
- The front door will not be seen (for shadow and sound only). So, we'd like a solid door, but it doesn't have to look any particular way.
- Completed set pieces will be moved into the wings of the theater for Evie to start sketching.
- We will be using Chris' white writing desk from Lend Me A Tenor.

Costumes:

- Catherine will have a bonnet and gloves to put on in Act II, scene 2.
  - We would like to find or make a reticule for Catherine that will match her dress in II.2.
- We would like a rehearsal jacket for Bob.
  - His jacket is very similar to a blazer. We will ask Bob if he has one he can bring in to start working with. If not, Costumes can have one for us by Sunday.
- Please stretch Bob's shoes as soon as possible so we can start rehearsing with them.
- We would like hoops and corsets fitted for rehearsal by Saturday.

Lighting:

- We will be having a sound meeting at 12 p.m. on Sunday, 7th.
- Hurricanes are in the rehearsal space; Jen will take some time to work with them and see how much light they will throw.

Sound:

- We will be having a sound meeting at 12 p.m. on Sunday, 7th.
- Rather than getting a doorbell, we would just like a doorknocker and we will adjust the line that refers to a doorbell.

Props:

- To obscure the clock face, we will try to find an ornate Victorian clock face and remove the hands.
  - If this doesn't work, we can just fog the glass with soap.
- The brandy glasses need to be more ornate.
- For the hurricanes, we will want ones that flare up or are straight cylinders (these are the safest).
- Final prop add date—Sunday, 7th.
- All of the chairs should be armless (the only exception being Dr Sloper's chair).

Appendix H.1
Production Meeting Notes

The Full Monty	Prod. Mtg. & Rehearsal Notes	
	DATE July 23, 2013	2 Blocks 1st Time Onstage

Please enjoy the entirety of the report, as several fascinating areas may apply to you.

General

*I need your photo call lists by the end of Saturday.

*Thank you for the stage time! It was very useful!

Scenic

*Can we actually write on the bathroom wall with lipstick?

*There is no good way to have a tire on the truck.

*We would like to cut the rail on the 4' x 4'.

Props

*We will use the large green box for both the coffin and sunbed—so we do not need to cover the entire 12' platform in card board, and the "funeral cloth" should also be appropriately sized.

*Jen will be taking the stripper photos.

*We would like a backpack for Nathan (Tony).

*The cooler should be the kind with a hinged, lift top rather than the slide top∧

*We would like a VERY long straw for Jeanette's drink

Costumes

*Thank you for seeing people today!

(Continued)

Continued

The Full Monty	Prod. Mtg. & Rehearsal Notes	
	DATE July 23, 2013	2 Blocks 1st Time Onstage

Lights

*We would like two spots and the personnel to operate them.

*We would like a small pool of light DSR for the transition cross on pg 24

Sound

*We need to record a preshow speech—we would like to use Sarah and try two different versions (Jeanette & Normal)

*We will need to have sound files for the two guitar licks in "Let it Go"

Music

*Brittany would like a list of the instrumentation to be used in the orchestra.

*Please let Zach know whether or not we want a drum shield after the orchestra rehearsal.

*Tim & Michael—we should think about which actors we want to use for percussion.

Stage Management

*There are no notes at this time.

Thank you,
The Full Monty Stage Management Team

Appendix I
Daily Sign-in

Show Name
Rehearsal Sign-In

Name 1	Name 2	Name 3

Name 4	Name 5	Name 6

Name 7	Name 8	Name 9

Name 10	Name 11	Name 12

Name 13	Name 14	Name 15

Appendix I.1
Tech and Performance Sign-in Sheet

	10/23/15 (5:00pm)	10/24/15 (5:00pm)	10/25/15 (12:00pm)	10/26/15 (12:00pm)	10/27/15 (OFF)	10/28/15 (5:00pm)	10/29/215 (5:00pm)	10/30/15 (5:00pm)	10/31/15 (5:00pm)	11/01/15 (12:00pm)	11/01/15 (6:00pm)	11/02/15 (12:00pm)
Alan H.												
Ann D.												
Anne S.												
Arianna R.												
Ashley M.												
Brittany R.												
Carolyn K.												
Claire M.												
Colleen W.												
Courtney P.												
Dakota G.												
Dana P.												
Danielle B.												
Elizabeth D.												
Erica B.												
Erin F.												
Eva S.												

Appendix J

Rehearsal Report

The Full Monty	Rehearsal Notes	
	DATE July 18, 2013	1 Block

Please enjoy the entirety of the report, as several fascinating areas may apply to you.

General

*Pg. 67 Change "Kate Smith" to "Liza."

*Pg. 70 Change Pam's line from "He looks more like you every day. He's gonna be a real heartbreaker" to "He's gonna be a real heartbreaker. Just like his father."

*Pg. 74 Malcolm's 1st line is in flux.

*Pg. 74 Harold's 2nd line should now read "Put that down, before you break it!"

*Pg. 77 Move "Anti Wrinkle cream . . . . . . it hasn't worked on Vicki" to after "This is what we're all supposed to look like, men and women"

*Pg. 77 Cut Harold's "Put it down, I said."

Scenic

*We would like to think about using the sofa (which folds down into a bed) as the bed rather than another wagon.

*The window treatment for "Harold's House" will need to be closed during the scene.

*We will only use two cabaret tables for The Goods.

*Let's talk railings.

(Continued)

Continued

The Full Monty	Rehearsal Notes	
	DATE July 18, 2013	1 Block

*The chair we are using for Jeanette (Sarah) at the piano should be one of the four cafeteria chairs.

*Three cafeteria trays.

*We will only use two cabaret tables and four chairs for The Goods.

*The backs of the mirror pieces will need to be dressed. They are visible to the audience.

Costumes

*Horse's (John) boxers should be blue.

Lights

*There are no notes at this time.

Sound

*There are no notes at this time.

Music

*There are no notes at this time.

Stage Management

*There are no notes at this time.

Thank you,
The Full Monty Stage Management Team

Appendix K
Line Notes

Character	Page	Error	Line as it should be
Connie	4	P	We barely have enough time to select and **prepare** for thirteen, I don't see how we can . . .
Connie	5	P	**How are we possibly going to review and** select 22 subjects. . . .
Connie	7	P	Well, **you're going to see that we** feature addicts who have. . . .
Connie	7	P	. . . support for the intervention, and they're more likely to **take** treatment.
Connie	7	P	Frankly, **he doesn't stand** much chance for recovery.
Connie	8	P	Many of them family of addicts, who **need to see** some glimmer of hope.
Connie	17	P	. . . we need to talk about Clemmy. **If we do go** with him, it's going to be a rough shoot.
Connie	19	SW	. . . I've **never had a** boss who'd **actually** done a shoot before. . . .
Connie	24	SK	. . . . "handle" shooting and coordinating **interventions for** 22 addicts a year . . .
Connie	25	SK, P	The **only** reason this show's a success . . . carefully choosing subjects and **arranging** their interventions . . .
Connie	26	P	. . . and the brother, and I've **left messages** for the long-lost father . . .
Connie	26	P	My red flags are turning into roadblocks. Brittany **will not allow the** father anywhere near Clemmy.
Connie	28	P	Gosh, Tara, until **you** got here . . . . to us that **our subjects were** vulnerable people who . . .
Connie	28	P	. . . that lets me determine **who can possibly make it.** . . . . . Be my guest. **You pick.** We need six more.
Connie	29	P	So we have to make DECISIONS. Really **hard** ones.

Error Key:	
P/Pa	Paraphrased
CL	Called Line
SK	Skipped word or phrase
SW	Switched word order
Add	Added word or phrase
Jump	Jumped someone else's line

Appendix L
Program Information Form

Program Information Form

Form must be typed and is due fourteen (14) calendar days BEFORE opening night.
Nicknames are NOT ACCEPTABLE for production credits.

Play Title: _____

Playwright: _____

Adaptor/Translator: _____

Book: _____

Lyrics: _____

Composer/Music: _____

Director: _____

Musical Director: _____

Choreographer: _____

Fight Choreographer: _____

Scene Design: _____

Costume Design: _____

Lighting Design: _____

Sound Design: _____

Production Dramaturge: _____

Provide SEPARATE sheets for EACH of the following:
CAST OF CHARACTERS
CAST AND CREW BIOGRAPHIES
TIME AND PLACE AND INTERMISSION (duration) INFORMATION
DIRECTOR'S/ PRODUCTION/ PROGRAM NOTES ORCHESTRA
PERSONNEL (if applicable)
ADVANCED PROJECTS (if applicable)

Note: Time and Place information is in regard to the <u>play's</u> locale and time period, NOT the theater location or performance time. For Musicals, the musical numbers must be listed within the Act/Scene breakdown, i.e.:

Scene 1 .... Outside Covent Garden
"Why Can't the English" .... Higgins
Scene 2 .... Higgins' Study
"The Rain in Spain" .... Eliza, Higgins

Production Staff

Note that not all positions will be filled for every production. Cross out what positions are not filled.

Stage Manager: _____

Assistant Stage Manager: _____

Assistant Director: _____

Dance Captain: _____

Fight Captain: _____

Rehearsal Accompanist: _____

Technical Director: _____

Assistant Technical Director: _____

Special Effects Designer: _____

Master Carpenter: _____

Master Electrician: _____

Property Master/Mistress: _____

Costumer: _____

Staff Costumer: _____

Wardrobe Master/Mistress: _____

Assistant(s) Choreographer: _____

Assistant(s) Scene Designer: _____

Assistant(s) Costume Designer: _____

Assistant(s) Lighting Designer: _____

Lightboard Operator: _____

Soundboard Operator: _____

House Manager: _____

Please add any other production staff positions and names as needed and in the appropriate sequence in the above list.

SPECIAL THANKS

(Relatives and friends are NOT thanked unless they have lent expertise, props, etc. directly to the production.)

<u>SPECIAL CIRCUMSTANCES (i.e. Smoking, Strobe Lights)</u>

<u>STANDARD PHRASES TO APPEAR IN ALL PROGRAMS</u> Please
silence all cell phones, pagers, and any other electronic devices.
Texting during productions will result in removal from the theatre.
The use of any recording device (photo, sound, or video) by audience members is not permitted.

<u>**Production Crews**</u>
List all names individually

Set Construction   Run Crew

Costume Construction   Costume Run Crew

Appendix L.1
Example Program Biography

Jonathan is excited to be returning for his second summer with the River Campus Summer Arts Festival. He is the lighting designer and technical director for the Department of Theatre and Dance. After this summer he heads off to the University of South Dakota's Department of Theatre to take over their lighting and sound design BFA and MFA program. Working both academically and professionally for over fifteen years, some of his recent work includes *The King and I*, *The Addams Family*, *Spring into Dance*, *Fall for Dance*, and *On the Town* for the Department of Theatre and Dance, and *Shear Madness*, *The Sound of Music*, and *A Wonderful Life* for Circa 21 Dinner Playhouse (www.aztheatricaldesign.com).

Photo Call List

THE FULL MONTY
Photo Call List

- Let it go—Final—LX 334
  - Platform USC horizontal (No railing), Square plat, 3 tables/chairs, clothing
  - The Goods—Mirror Moment—LX 238
  - 2 tables/chairs, couch (Harold's), SR wall in Harold's house
  - During, Set Jerry's clothes for Breeze
- Breeze off the River—"Sometimes I Feel"—LX 220
  - Flip SR wall to Jerry's house, Couch (Jerry's)
  - End of "Woman's World"—LX 64
  - SR and SL Walls on (SR add stall wall, strike curtains)
  - During, set bed for "You Rule My World"
- "You Rule My World"—LX168
  - Walls off, Bed on
- Keno @ the light wall—LX 14
  - Platform in runway (with stairs), 3 tables/chairs, square plat, mic Paper throw in Scrap—LX 34
  - Platform DSR, square plat w/ 2 stairs, paper
- Life with Harold
  - Platform Horizontal + railing
  - During, set truck in wing Beer Chat in Big Ass Rock—LX 110
  - Truck on
  - During, set Caleb's security guard costume Michael Jordan's Ball—Circle—LX 184
  - Table on (USL), Piano
- Show Biz Number Button—LX 208
  - Prep coffin
- End of "Walk with Me"—LX 274
  - Platform DSC (No railing), coffin
  - During, set stripper outfits for all boys
- Man—"What is a Man? Why Does He Bother?" Jerry—LX 82
  - Transition
- "Let it Go"—Jerry jump over Dave—LX 320
  - Platform in runway (No stairs), square platform "Let it Go"—Ties—LX 322
- "Let it Go"—Belts—LX 324

Appendix N
Preshow Checklist

UPON ARRIVAL TO BUILDING (At least 15 Minutes prior to the call time)	
	Turn on house lights
	Unlock house doors
	Turn on hallway lights
	Upstage left door keyed open and held open
	Turn on stair lights by dressing rooms and green room
Women's Dressing Room	
	Unlock doors
	Turn on hall light, mirror lights, bathroom lights, & power to dressing tables
	Monitor volumes set to: ____
Men's Dressing Room	
	Unlock doors
	Turn on hall light, mirror lights, bathroom lights, & power to dressing tables
Green Room	
	Monitor volumes set to: ____
	Unlock both doors
	Turn on lights
	Monitor volume set to: ____
Rehearsal Studio	
	Unlock doors
	Turn on lights
Light Booth	
	Unlock door
	Turn on overhead lights
	Unlock and open window
Sound Booth	
	Prop open door
	Turn on overhead lights
	Unlock and open window
	Turn on stage manager running lights
	Stage manager monitor volume set to: ____

(Continued)

Continued

6:00pm (12:30pm)	
	Check attendance on sign-in sheet and call latecomers
	Preset all off-stage props, gels, etc. (ASMs / crew) (see prop preset)
	Sweep and mop hall leading to dressing rooms and green room (ASMs / crew)
	Confirm that light and sound checks are underway
	Check here when light operator has notified you that light check is complete
	Check here when sound operator has notified you that sound check is complete
6:30pm (1:00pm)	
	Call "15 minutes to vocal warm-up"
	Check in with the house manager
	Inspect glow tape and fix if necessary
	Inspect spike marks and fix if necessary
	Sweep and mop the stage (make sure floor is sealed) (ASMs / crew)
	Vacuum all carpet (ASMs / crew)
6:45pm (1:15pm)	
	Call "Vocal warm-up"
	Preset all onstage furniture, props, etc. (ASMs / crew) (see prop preset)
	Check run lights
6:55pm (1:25pm)	
	Call "5 minutes until house opens—check your props"
	Turn off overhead lights in light booth, sound booth, and hallway
	Shut booth doors & windows (leave unlocked)
	Call preshow light and sound cues
	Make sure works are off and board has control of the house
	Confirm with house manager that you are ready to open house in five minutes
7:00pm (1:30pm)	
	Make sure the stage is clear
	Notify House Manager that you are ready to open house
	Call "Half-hour and house is open"
7:15pm (1:45pm)	
	Call "15 minutes"
	Collect Valuables
	Check in with the house manager
7:25pm (1:55pm)	
	Call "5 minutes—crew to places"
	Confirm with House Manager that you are ready for house to close in 5 minutes
	Crew to places
	Green room lights off

7:28pm (1:58pm)	
	Call "Places"
7:30pm (2:00pm)	
	Confirm with house manager that house is closed
	Confirm that all performers and any preshow presenters are in place
	Start the show (don't forget to start your stopwatch)

Appendix N.1
Props Checklist

Who	Prop	PRESET/Notes	
	Stage Right		
	Money	Table	✔
	UGC Desk	Poppins Counter	✔
	UGC Chair	Black Leather	✔
	Shovel	In Corner	✔
	3 Flashlights		✔
	3 Plastic Billy Clubs		✔
	Pile of Faxes		✔
	2 Mugs		✔
	Big Red Mug		✔
	Nail File		✔
	Blindfold		✔
	Rope for Bobby		✔
	4 Signs (Slain, Killed, Specter, Hero)		✔
	Tickets		✔
	Onstage		
	Amenity Table	Yellow Spike	✔
	Ledger	On Table	✔
	Coin Box	On Table	✔
	Amenity Chair	Yellow Spike	✔
	Cleaning Bucket	Downstage of desk	✔
	Death Sign	By Band	✔
	Stage Left		
	Cleaning Supplies		✔
	Mop		✔
	Broom		✔
	Money / Black Clip		✔
	3 Flashlights		✔
	3 Plastic Billy Clubs		✔

	"Fee Hike" Poster	✔
	Pee Free Banner/Flag	✔
	Script	✔
	Black Coffee Cup	✔
	Makeup and Brush	✔
	Blush	✔
	Sunglasses	✔
	Nail Polish	✔
	Pamphlets	✔
	Armless Wooden Chair	✔
	Rope for Hope	✔
	Gag	✔
	Briefcase	✔
Stage Left		
	Money	✔
	3 Signs (Villian, Ghost, Murdered)	✔
	Tickets	✔
Personal Props		
	Little Sally Coin Bag	✔
	Lockstock Billy Club	✔
	Barrel Billy Club	✔
	Lockstock Flashlight	✔
	Barrel Flashlight	✔
	Fipp Bundle of Cash	✔
	Key	✔
	Little Sally Stuffed Dog	✔

Appendix O
Sample Run Sheet

Who:	Task:	What:	Where:	When:	Notes:
				Top Of Show	
	Sweep	Deck			
	Mop	Deck			
	Set	Props SL			
	Set	Props SR			
	Set	Props Onstage	SL		
	Fly In	Amenity Flat	Line 5		
	Fly In	Amenity Masking	Line 13		
	Places / Cue	SL—Gretchen, Josh, Gabby, Andrew, Anna, Spencer, Jeff			
	Places / Cue	SR—Abby, Gabrielle, Deanna, Amelia, Will, Michelle, Jack, Vallen, Devann, Cassandra, Emma, Micah, Lorina, Casey			
	Places / Cue	HL—Ben, Sam, Moriah, Olivia, Arielle			
				During I.1	
Morgan	Catch	Broom	SL		
Morgan	Handoff	Mop	SL		
Austin	Prep	UGC Desk	SR	"The politicians taxed the toilets"	
Austin	Prep	UGC Chair	SR	"The politicians taxed the toilets"	
				Into I.2 to UGC—"Mr. Cladwell"—Shift Red	
Austin	Fly Out	Amenity Masking	Line 13	S.M. GO	Grid—Pace with wall
Morgan	Fly Out	Amenity Wall	Line 5	"	Grid—10 count
Rob	Fly In	UGC Sign	Line 8	"	Green Spikes
Josh & Amelia	Strike	Amenity Table	> SL	B/O	"
Gretchen	Strike	Amenity Chair	> SL		"
Deanna	Strike	Cleaning Supplies	> SL		"
Andrew & Jeff	Set	UGC Desk	< SR	Able	
Micah	Set	UGC Chair	< SR		"

(Continued)

During I.2

			SL	Upon Exit	
Ellery	Quick Change	Vallen Poor to Rich	SL	Upon Exit	≈ 45 seconds
Moriah	Quick Change	Amelia Poor to Rich	SR	"	≈ 45 seconds

Into I.3 to the Street—Shift Blue

Rob	Fly Out	UCG Sign	Line 8	S.M. GO	Blue Spikes
Spencer & Andrew	Strike	UGC Desk	> SR	B/O	
Micah	Strike	UGC Chair	> SR	"	

Into I.4 to the Amenity—Shift Violet

Morgan	Fly In	Amenity Wall	Line 5	S.M. GO	
Austin	Fly In	Amenity Masking	Line 13	"	
Gabrielle & Jeff	Set	Amenity Table	< SL	Able	w/ Ledger, Pen, and Cash Box
Gretchen	Set	Amenity Chair	< SL	"	

Into I.5 to UGC—Pink

Morgan	Fly Out	Amenity Wall	Line 5	S.M. GO	Grid—10 count
Austin	Fly Out	Amenity Masking	Line 13	"	Grid—Pace with wall
Rob	Fly In	UGC Sign	Line 8	"	Green Spikes
Abby & Will	Strike	Amenity Table	> SL	B/O	

Appendix P
Post-Show Checklist

City of Angels

- ☐ Turn on hex lights
- ☐ Turn off run lights
- ☐ Twist on stage door lights, Twist off stage door run light
- ☐ Twist on SL stair lights
- ☐ Turn off hazer
- ☐ Check projector is off
- ☐ Bring in "performance in progress" sign
- ☐ Put away props
- ☐ Put away furniture
- ☐ Turn on compressor
- ☐ Lock gates
- ☐ Plug phones back in
     Jonathan's office
     Dennis' office
     Sarah's desk
- ☐ Return headsets
- ☐ Close costume shop (unless costumes are being laundered)
- ☐ Close scene shop
- ☐ Close guys' dressing room (unless costumes will be returned)
- ☐ Close girls' dressing room (unless costumes will be returned)
- ☐ Lock prop cabinet
- ☐ Put out ghost light
- ☐ Sign out

Appendix Q
Calling Script Example

And thou oppos'd, being of no woman born,
Yet I will try the last. Before my body,
I throw my warlike Shield: Lay on Macduff,
And damn'd be him, that first cries hold, enough.

Exit fighting. Alarums Enter fighting, and MACBETH slain ~~ON 1ST BACK~~ HIT *LQ280*

Enter MALCOLM, ROSSE, ANGUS, and OLD SIWARD

MALCOLM
I would the Friends we miss, were safe arriv'd. ~~SCENE Light~~ *LQ285*

SIWARD
Some must go off: and yet by these I see,
So great a day as this is cheaply bought.

MALCOLM
Macduff is missing, and your Noble Son.

ROSSE
Your son my Lord, ha's paid a soldier's debt.

Enter MACDUFF

MACDUFF
Hail King, for so thou art.
Behold, where lies   STANDBY
Th'Usurpers cursed head: the time is free: LQ 290 - 310
I see thee compast with thy Kingdoms Pearl,   AND WITCHES
That speak my salutation in their minds: LANTERNS OUT
Whose voices I desire aloud with mine.
Hail King of Scotland.

ALL
Hail King of Scotland.

MALCOLM
We shall not spend a large expense of time,
Before we reckon with your several loves,
And make us even with you. My Thanes and Kinsmen
Henceforth be Earls, the first that ever Scotland   CLIP LIGHT
In such an Honor nam'd: What's more to do,   OUT
Which would be planted newly with the time,
As calling home our exil'd Friends abroad,
That fled the Snares of watchful Tyranny,
Producing forth the cruel Ministers
Of this dead Butcher, and his Fiend-like Queen;
Who (as 'tis thought) by self and violent hands,
Took off her life. This, and what needful else
That call's upon us, by the Grace of Grace,
We will perform in measure, time, and place: (DARK FOR)
So thanks to all at once, and to each one,   ML5   WITCHES
Whom we invite, to see us Crown'd at Scone. C TO LEAVE   LQ290

End of play.

                    WITCHES SWITCH
                    LANTERNS OFF
              (ALEX → AYANA → BRUCE)
                    Ⓓ (FL) BLOW OUT CANDLE   LQ300
                    CURTAIN CALL   LQ305
                    POST SHOW   LQ310
                    HOUSE LIGHTS,
                         UP (SLIDER)

Appendix R
Performance Report

The Full Monty			
Date: August 2nd, 2013		**Show Number: 7**	
Today's Schedule: 7:30 p.m. Go		**Next Performance: Saturday, August 3rd, 7:30 p.m.**	
Curtain Speech Recorded	**Act I** 7:38 p.m.–8:52 p.m.; 1:14:43	**Intermission** 8:52 p.m.–9:10 p.m.; 18min	**Act 2** 9:10 p.m.–10:09 p.m.; 0:59:01

Performance Evaluation: * A completely sold-out house and great energy from the cast. * Lots of laughter and applause. Overall a solid performance. We received a standing ovation.	**Actor Notes:** * Jeff—pg. 32—para—"Malcolm! Right, right." * Jeff—pg. 96—Skip—It's nothing to do with another woman, all right?
Sound: * Sarah's mic was cutting in and out during "Show Biz Number"	**Lights:** * LX 142 was late—Reg's strip * LX 144 was late—Out of Reg's strip * LX 200 was late—Top of Show Biz Number
Costumes: * None	**Props:** * None
Scenic/Paint: * Please look at the traveller; closing it the final couple of feet has become difficult (it was hit by the truck) * Caleb's belt flew into the lamppost during the transition. It knocked into the top and set it askew. (Jonathan fixed this before cabaret)	**Administrative Notes:** * We are out of hand soap; both front of house and in the cast bathroom.
Music (if a musical) or Script (any changes): * There are no notes at this time.	**Other Notes:** * 1st Crash SR got tangled * The picture on Harold's wall was very crooked tonight * The mid-stage traveler was not quite closed at the end of the dress rehearsal

Performance Report Example 2

Our Country's Good
STAGE MANAGER'S PERFORMANCE REPORT
Performance #8—Friday, October 7

Running Times/Figures:

- **House Count:** 85 people
- **House Open:** 7:00 p.m.
- **Curtain Up:** 7:32 p.m.
- **Act I:** 1 hour, 17 minutes
- **Intermission:** 15 minutes
- **Act II:** 1 hour, 5 minutes
- **Curtain Down:** 10:12 p.m.

Performance Notes:

- Prior to the performance, it came to my attention that several times throughout the run, including tonight, the actors had received costumes that were still damp at call. Quite a few actors were understandably complaining about this. I spoke to Nikki about this after the show and explained that they needed to receive costumes that were completely dry.
- Will was very briefly late for his entrance in I.4 because the glasses he was supposed to bring on had not been washed and he had to scramble to get clean glasses for a different scene. It was not noticeable.
- Ben did say his line "You will get much praise as Brazen, Wisehammer" (II.11) but he also skipped Sideway's line "We'll use it in the Sideway Theatre" in the process.
- Tonight was an excellent performance, one of our best yet, and we had a fantastic audience who really enjoyed the show.

Sets:

- One of the pieces of black fabric hanging in the DS stairwell (next to the booth) is falling down. We tried to tape it back up but it was not staying. Could you please look at this?

Props:

- Could we get another leaf for the fan? The one we have is currently being held together by gaff tape.

Lights:

- No notes at this time.

Sound:

- No notes at this time.

Costumes:

- Adam's Phillip coat is still missing a button.
- Prior to the performance, it came to my attention that several times throughout the run, including tonight, the actors had received costumes that were still damp at call. Quite a few actors were understandably complaining about this. I spoke to Nikki about this after the show and explained that they needed to receive costumes that were completely dry.

Thanks!
Stage Management

Online Resources

There are so many different resources in existence today, an entire book could be written on just online resources, how to use them, and their purpose. We wanted to give you a brief overview of some resources that we or some close colleagues have used to help keep up with the production process and the ever-changing technological needs of a production. As Apple users we can only give you the briefest of information on PC-based apps and programs, but we encourage you to use sites and apps as a resource for finding or creating things that work best for you and your process.

Theatrical Resources

Actors Equity Association (www.actorsequity.org)
American Guild of Musical Artists (www.musicalartists.org)
American Guild of Variety Artists (www.agvausa.com/)
ArtsJournal (www.artsjournal.com)
Control Booth (www.controlbooth.com)
IATSE (www.iatse-intl.org)
Offstage Jobs (http://offstagejobs.com)
Screen Actors Guild—American Federation of Television and Radio Artists (www.sagaftra.org/)
SM Network (www.smnetwork.org)
SM Toolkit and National Survey (www.sm-sim.com/)
Society of American Fight Directors (www.safd.org/)
Stage Directors and Choreographers Society (www.sdcweb.org)
Stage Managers Association (www.stagemanagers.org)
Theatre Communications Group (www.tcg.org)
United States Institute for Theatre Technology (www.usitt.org)
Virtual Callboard (www.virtualcallboard.com)

Meetings and Scheduling

Doodle (www.Doodle.com): Need to coordinate everyone's schedule to find a common time to have a meeting? Doodle allows you to send out a list of times and collates everyone's responses into easy-to-read data noting the time everyone is free.

Free Conference Call (www.FreeConferenceCall.com): A great way to set up a free voice conference call between multiple parties in different locations. New features include video conferencing as well.

Google Calendars (www.google.com/calendar): Online calendars. Create and share a rehearsal schedule, create a schedule for yourself with reminders, or share a tech schedule with the design team. Google makes calendars easy to create and share.

Meeting Wizard (www.Meetingwizard.com): Very similar to Doodle, Meeting Wizard allows you to send out a list of times and collates everyone's responses into easy-to-read data noting the time everyone is free. Meeting Wizard can also be used to announce a meeting that is already scheduled or send reminders about scheduled meetings.

Cloud Storage

Amazon Cloud Drive (www.amazon.com/clouddrive/home)
Dropbox (www.dropbox.com)
Google Drive (drive.google.com)

Other Productivity

These apps are available online through most Web browsers, allowing you to access the information on almost any computer no matter the operating system as long as you have an Internet connection. Most of these apps also have a mobile version, as well as apps for both iOS and Android.

Checkvist (www.checkvist.com): An online checklist app that allows you to create a list and share it. Any of your shared users can check off things on the list or see what has been checked off, and the program stores when something was checked off and by whom. This app also allows for nesting (the ability to give any item a sub-category). There are some additional features that a monthly or yearly subscription unlocks, but these are not necessary to use this resource very functionally.

Evernote (Evernote.com): A great note-taking and collaboration app to take and share notes.

Google Hangouts (hangouts.google.com): A good way to group video chat with team members no matter their location as long as everyone has a decent Internet connection.

Google Maps (maps.google.com): A great tool that allows you to find your way to any number of things, as well as search for dining options, medical resources, or transit options.

Remind (www.remind.com): A great way to communicate quickly and easily with your entire cast and design team. Set up multiple "classes," one for your actors and rehearsal contacts and another for your design team, so you can quickly send out information without having to add everyone's information every time. This is for quick updates and reminders, not long communiqués. This was designed for communication between teachers and classes without needing to give out a personal phone number, but works very well for theatrical purposes.

Skype (www.skype.com): A good way to group chat or group video chat when production meetings need to take place with team members spread out around the country. This does require a decent Internet connection and some features require payment.

Wunderlist (http://wunderlist.com): A checklist app that allows users to create a list and share it with multiple people, and set reminders and deadlines.

IOS Apps

Alarmed ~ Reminders + Timers by Yoctoville: Need to record the time on several different things at once? This app can do that, in addition to setting both time- and location-based reminders.

Amazon Cloud Drive by Amazon: A cloud-based storage app, which also has an online app.

ETC iRFR-Preview by Electronic Theatre Controls Inc.: The iRFR allows you to watch the cue list of any ETC EOS family console. There is a slight delay between the app and the console, so do not depend on it for calling cues.

Evernote by Evernote: A great note-taking and collaboration app to take and share notes.

Dropbox by Dropbox: A cloud-based storage app that has a desktop app and an online app.

Genius Scan by The Grizzly Lab: A quick and easy way to scan a document, whiteboard, receipt, etc. using just your phone's camera. The free version doesn't allow all export features, but does allow e-mail. The paid version unlocks all features.

Google Drive by Google: A cloud-based storage app that links with Google's document suite. This app also has a desktop app and an online app.

Google Maps by Google: A great GPS app that allows you to find your way to any number of things.

*__iAnnotate__ by Branchfire Inc: A very handy PDF annotator that allows for the use of many different annotation tools, Dropbox sync, and sharing.

iRigging by J.R. Clancy, Inc.: An app that gives you rigging information and calculations.

*__Qlab Remote__ by Figure 53: A remote for the Mac app Qlab, which shows the cue stack as well as allowing minor edits of levels and stopping or starting cues.

Remind: Safe Classroom Communication by Remind 101: A great way to communicate quickly and easily with your entire cast and design team. This is for quick updates and reminders, not long communiqués. This was designed for communication between teachers and classes without needing to give out a personal phone number, but works very well for theatrical purposes. It also has an online app.

Scannable by Evernote: A quick and easy way to scan a document, whiteboard, receipt, etc. using just your phone's camera. You can then sync to Evernote or e-mail it to yourself.

Skype by Microsoft: A free way to group chat or group video chat. This does require a decent Internet connection.

*Stage Write** by Open Jar Productions LLC: An app to record blocking and choreography. This app is expensive but is very helpful for creating nice blocking sheets, especially for choreography. It is not the fastest app to work in, so recording blocking by hand first and then inputting the information later may be the way to go.

*Step Timer** by West Side Systems: Allows you to count beats per minute as well as calculate the time between each step (the beats or movements in choreography, etc.).

*Take 10!** by Wooly: A great app to calculate breaks during rehearsals using Actors' Equity Association rules.

*time:calc** by Watten Earth: An app to help you calculate all those pesky times from rehearsals and performances.

Wunderlist by Wunderlist: A checklist app that allows users to create a list and share that list with multiple people, and set reminders and deadlines.

* = paid app

Mac Apps

multistopwatch.com: An online stopwatch useful for timing individual acts as well as the entire show (lap and split times).

Nocturne: An app that will darken your screen so you can have it open in tech and not distract others.

Wunderlist (www.wunderlist.com/): A checklist app that allows users to create a list and share that list with multiple people, and set reminders and deadlines.

PC Apps

Mega-Watch (www.willpickens.com/megawatch_index.html): A time-keeping and break timer.

multistopwatch.com: An online stopwatch useful for timing individual acts as well as the entire show (lap and split times).

Wunderlist (www.wunderlist.com/): A checklist app that allows users to create a list and share that list with multiple people, and set reminders and deadlines.

Suggested Readings

A Method for Lighting the Stage
  Stanley McCandless
  ISBN-10: 0878300821

Backwards and Forwards: A Technical Manual for Reading Plays
  David Ball
  ISBN-10: 0809311100

Crucial Conversations: Tools for Talking When Stakes Are High
  Kerry Patterson, Joseph Grenny, Ron McMillan, Al Switzler
  ISBN-10: 0071771328

Designing with Light, 6th Edition
  J. Michael Gillette
  ISBN-10: 0073514233

Einstein's Dreams
  Alan Lightman
  ISBN-10: 9781400077809

Essentials of Stage Management
  Peter Maccoy
  ISBN-10: 0878301992

Fierce Conversations: Achieving Success at Work and in Life One Conversation at a Time
  Susan Scott
  ISBN-10: 0425193373

Getting to Yes: Negotiating Agreement Without Giving In (Paperback—May 3, 2011)
  Roger Fisher, William Ury, Bruce Patton
  ISBN-10: 0143118757

Great Directors at Work: Stanislavsky, Brecht, Kazan, Brook
  David Richard Jones
  ISBN-10: 0520061748

How to Manage Meetings
  Alan Barker
  ISBN-10: 0749463422

Illustrated Theatre Production Guide, 3rd Edition
  John Holloway
  ISBN-10: 0415717523

On Directing
  Harold Clurman
  ISBN-10: 0684826224

Producing Theatre: A Comprehensive Legal and Business Guide, 3rd Edition
  Donald C. Farber
  ISBN-10: 0879103175

Script Analysis for Actors, Directors, and Designers
  James Thomas
  ISBN-10: 0415663253

S.M.Arts Guidelines: Stage Managing the Arts in Canada
  Winston Morgan
  ISBN-10: 0968744400

Stagecraft Fundamentals, 2nd Edition
  Rita Carver
  ISBN-10: 0240820517

Stage Makeup, 10th Edition
  Richard Corson, James Glavan, Beverly Gore Norcross
  ISBN-10: 0205644546

Stage Management: The Essential Handbook
  Gail Pallin
  ISBN-10: 1848420145

Stage Manager: The Professional Experience
  Larry Fazio
  ISBN-10: 0240804104

Stage Management Forms and Formats
  Barbara Dilker
  ISBN-10: 0896762289

The Stage Rigging Handbook, 3rd Edition
  Jay O. Glerum
  ISBN-10: 0809327414

The Arts Management Handbook: New Directions for Students and Practitioners
   Meg Brindle, Constance DeVereaux
   ISBN-10: 0765617420

Theatrical Design and Production: An Introduction to Scene Design and Construction, Lighting Sound, Costume and Makeup, 7th Edition
   J. Michael Gillette
   ISBN-10: 0073382221

The Back Stage Guide to Stage Management
   Thomas A. Kelly
   ISBN-10: 0823098028

The Backstage Handbook
   Paul Carter
   ISBN-10: 0911747397

Technical Theatre for Nontechnical People, 2nd Edition
   Drew Cambell
   ISBN-10: 1581153449

The Definitive Book of Body Language
   Barbara Pease and Allan Pease
   ISBN-10: 0553804723

The Director's Voice
   Arthur Bartow
   ISBN-10: 0930452747

The Dramatic Imagination
   Robert Edmond Jones
   ISBN-10: 0878301844

The Poetics
   Aristotle
   ISBN-10: 0140446362

The Stage Management Handbook
   Daniel Ionazzi
   ISBN-10: 1558702350

The Stage Manager's Toolkit: Templates and Communication Techniques to Guide Your Theatre Production from First Meeting to Final Performance (The Focal Press Toolkit Series)
   Laurie Kincman
   ISBN-10: 0415663199

Working Together in Theatre: Collaboration and Leadership
   Robert Cohen
   ISBN-10: 023023982X

Index

References to figures are shown in *italics*.

and concept meetings 7, 53; and cue-to-cue rehearsals 89–90; and daily rehearsal schedules 43; director check-in (after rehearsal) 71; and meetings, running 55–6; and meeting schedules 54; and music rehearsals 59; and paper or dry techs 84; and photo calls 76, 77; and pre-opening night checks 99; and production calendars 42–3; and prop lists 14; and rehearsal props/furniture 49; and rehearsal reports 64, 71; and rehearsals, starting and running 63; and rehearsal schedules 42, 43; and rehearsal space prepping 44; role of 21; and run sheets 79–80; and stage managers 3, 4, 5, 21, 63, 103; and stage managers, first meeting with 25–6; and technical notes 67–8, 95; and tech rehearsals 86, 89; and video recordings for blocking notes 67; and workstations 61; and world of the play 7, 21; *see also* artistic directors (ADs); music directors; technical directors (TDs)

discretion: quality of good stage manager 6; *see also* gossip

Disney, *Alice in Wonderland* 7

Doodle 17, 194

downstage 10

dramaturges 24

dressing rooms 24, 28, 77, 92

dress rehearsals: costume quick change rehearsals 91–2; onstage crew in costumes 93; photo calls 77; postshow actor and tech notes 95; postshow cleanup 95; preset checklists 79, 93–4; preshow setup/checks 93–4; staff on headsets during 91

Dropbox 16, 194, 195

dry techs 84

electricians 81, 91; master electricians 54, 86, 98

e-mail communication 54, 57, 71

emergency procedures 27, 31–2; emergency contact forms 62; medical emergency 32

environmental (or site-specific) theaters 9

Equity *see* Actors' Equity Association

Euripides, *Iphigenia at Aulis* character breakdown 145–7

Excel template, for preliminary notes 11

expendables (or perishable props) 14

fast costume changes (or quick changes) 80, 92

Febreeze spray 97

fights: fight calls 94; fight captains 98; fight choreographers 23, 94, 98, 99

fines 16, 44

fire, and safety 33

first aid: courses 33; first aid kits 31, 61

flexibility, quality of good stage manager 5

fly crews 24, 91

flying scenery 24, 80, 84

food: dietary requirements 62; as expendables (or perishable props) 14; food service hours in academic setting and rehearsal scheduling 42

"fourth wall" concept 9

framing squares 47

French scene breakdowns 14, 40; example 138

front of house 56, 74, 92, 94, 101–2; house managers 29, 32, 91, 101

The Full Monty: performance report 189; photo call list 173–4; production meeting and rehearsal notes 157–8; rehearsal notes 163–4

full tech rehearsals 89, 90

furniture: furniture list 40; rehearsal furniture 49, 60; and spiking at rehearsals 69–71, *70*; storage areas 29; and tape out of rehearsal space 44

gaffers tape 15, 61

gel colors 22

glow gaff tape 81

glow spikes 82

glow tape 15, 71, 81, 82

gobos 22

God mics 91

Good Television, line notes example 165–6

Google Calendars 17, 194

Google Docs/Drive 16, 194, 195

Google Sites 17

gossip 3; *see also* discretion

"GO" word, and talking on headset 92

Grease, rehearsal schedule 149–50

Greek theatre 8

green rooms: and callboards 28; and costume quick changes 92; and headset protocol 91

groundplans 46, *47*, 48, 64, 66, *66*

hair/wig designers 22, 85

hand props 13, 29

headsets: headset protocol 90; and word "GO" 92

headshots 75

The Heiress, production meeting agenda 155–6

hex key sets 15

house: definitions 101; opening the house 101–2; *see also* front of house

house counts 101

house managers 29, 32, 91, 101; *see also* front of house

humor, quality of good stage manager 6

IATSE (International Alliance of Theatrical Stage Employees) 86

injury reporting 31, 33, 63

interviews (to promote the show) 76

keys: booths (control rooms) 28; and load-in 79; and stage managers 29; weaponry cases 31

kneepads 50